PELICAN BOOKS
A115
PREHISTORIC BRITAIN
JACQUETTA AND CHRISTOPHER HAWKES

PREHISTORIC BRITAIN

*

JACQUETTA AND
CHRISTOPHER HAWKES

PENGUIN BOOKS

HARMONDSWORTH · MIDDLESEX

Penguin Books Ltd, Harmondsworth, Middlesex
U.S.A.: Penguin Books Inc, 3300 Clipper Mill Road, Baltimore 11, Md
[*Educational Representative:*
D. C. Heath & Co, 285 Columbus Avenue, Boston 16, Mass]
AUSTRALIA: Penguin Books Pty Ltd, 200 Normanby Road,
Melbourne, S.C.5, Victoria
AGENT IN CANADA: Riverside Books Ltd, 47 Green Street,
Saint Lambert, Montreal, P.Q.

—

Collogravure plates printed by
Harrison and Sons Ltd, London

—

Made and printed in Great Britain by
Hunt, Barnard and Company Ltd, London and Aylesbury

—

First published 1937
Published in Penguin Books 1943
Reprinted 1949, 1952

Acknowledgements

We desire gratefully to acknowledge permission given by the following institutions, authors, and publishers for the reproduction of illustrations:

Ashmolean Museum, Oxford (pls. 8, 14, 15); British Museum (pls. 2c, 3, 5, 9, 10, 13, 16b; figs. 8, 15, 17, 19); Mr M. C. Burkitt, F.S.A., and the Cambridge University Press (fig. 2); Mrs Burkitt and Prof. V. Gordon Childe, F.S.A. (fig. 3); Cambridge University Museum of Archæology and Ethnology (pls. 2b, 16a); Dr J. G. D. Clark, F.S.A. and Messrs Methuen & Co, Ltd (fig. 18); Dr E. Cecil Curwen, F.S.A., and the same (figs. 4, 6); Mr W. J. Hemp, F.S.A. (pl. 1a); Dr P. Jacobsthal, Hon. F.S.A. (pls. 11, 12); Mr Alexander Keiller, F.S.A. (pls. 4a, 7); Central Office of Information and Ministry of Education (pl. 4b, taken by Mr Walter Bird); Oxford University Press (fig. 7); Mr C. W. Phillips, F.S.A. (pl. 2a, fig. 9); Prehistoric Society (fig. 13); Royal Commission on Ancient Monuments, Scotland (pl. 6, fig. 20).

Fig. 1 has been specially drawn for this book, from originals in Mr M. C. Burkitt's collection, by Mrs Burkitt, to whom we offer our particular thanks.

C. F. C. H.

Contents

List of Plates

LIST OF PLATES

A TABLE OF DATES

THE reader will understand that the earlier these are, the less precise their accuracy becomes. Dates before about 10,000 B.C. are only rough indications; thence on to about 2000 B.C. they are (for Britain) simple approximations; thereafter, broadly speaking, they get gradually more and more accurate until exact historical dating begins with Caesar's expeditions and the Roman conquest of the 1st century A.D.

Speaking generally, the basis of the earlier dates is geological (in part also astronomical); the later ones are for the most part based ultimately upon the known chronologies of contemporary Egypt, Mesopotamia, Greece, or Rome.

	B.C.
Palaeolithic period, beginning	about 550,000
Aurignacian replaces Neanderthal Man	about 100,000
Palaeolithic period giving place ⎱ to Mesolithic period ⎰	⎰ about 12,000– ⎱ 10,000
Maglemose culture flourishing ⎱ Britain becomes an island ⎰	about 6000
Dawn of civilization in the Near East	about 6000–5000
In Britain:–	
Neolithic period beginning	2300
Early Bronze Age: Beaker invasions	1900–1800
Early Bronze Age: Wessex invasion	1500
Middle Bronze Age: rise of Urn people beginning	1300
Late Bronze Age beginning	900
Late Bronze Age: Deverel-Rimbury invasions	750
Early Iron Age beginning	450–400
Early Iron Age: La Tène invasions beginning	250
Early Iron Age: Belgic invasions in Kent	75
Julius Caesar's expeditions	55 and 54
Early Iron Age: Belgic invasion of Commius	50

	A.D.
Cunobelin becomes king at Camulodunum (Colchester)	10
Roman conquest begins under Claudius	43

Foreword

IN a single century archaeology has pushed the beginning of human history back some half million years, and given it a perspective which was altogether lacking when knowledge was restricted to the comparatively short span of time covered by written records. And the material with which the prehistorian works is far more intimate than the documents of the historian. It is true that he lacks the romantic appeal of famous names, he cannot marshal an array of kings, heroes and law-givers, but instead he handles the actual things which helped men to pass their lives: the pots from which they ate and drank, the weapons with which they hunted or killed one another, their houses, their hearthstones and their graves. Such material keeps him much closer to the essentials of history. He must be concerned with the lives and achievements of countless ordinary, anonymous people.

Archaeology has enabled us to understand how, from the moment when primitive human creatures shaped the first tools, chapter after chapter has been added to the tale of man's accomplishments. He masters fire, he discovers a mechanical principle, he becomes an artist, he learns to farm, to weave, to shape pots, to sail boats, to make wheels, to cast bronze, to work iron, until imperceptibly we have reached the unfinished chapter of to-day. There is no break in this procession of events. For myself, I always see them as it were threaded on a taut line which stretches from the present near my eyes back and back into the distance of the past – a line which is in fact the historical time-sequence, the long line of the passing years. Because we are so conscious of this thread of time running through history, we have in this book held to it as a guide, following beside it for the tens of thousands

11

of years that lead from eoliths to the Romans. A pedestrian method certainly, but one which keeps the vast complex story in good order and helps to convey the sense of continuity between the past, present and future of humanity, which is the underlying theme.

This book wishes to be no more than the briefest chronicle of the way that he went in the small but never unimportant corner of the world that we have come to know as the British Isles.

A word on the manner of our collaboration. I have written chapters I-IV, the greater part of V and have added the tailpiece. My husband wrote certain parts of the Vth and the whole of the VIth chapters. More than that, his exacting scholar's eye scanned my text and allowed nothing dubious or inaccurate to pass. For this the reader will be more grateful than I was.

J. J. H.

Prelude

I BEGAN upon the first edition of this book in 1940, when, if one listened to the intellect alone, a German victory seemed almost certain. I was in fact preparing to write about the deepest roots of a civilization whose topmost shoots were perhaps soon to be hacked off. Seeking a justification for this fiddle-playing, I was able to suggest that although my subject was remote in time, there was yet something topical in it. There was a sudden probability that the pattern of prehistoric events would be repeated, and that the repetition would be imposed upon one's own life. As this book will show, prehistorians had spent much learning and ingenuity on reconstructing thousand-year-old stories of continental invasions of Britain. In 1940 we awaited a practical demonstration in modern form.

It was amusing to see in how many ways the present promised to mirror the past: it was even reassuring – the feeling 'this has happened before' gave perspective to one's own fate. In the early summer of the year I was living in East Anglia, where it was known that we were threatened from the Low Countries, North Germany and Scandinavia, just the regions from which the prehistoric invaders of our Eastern coasts had usually come. Archaeological authority concurred: in early times the eastern counties were always open to invasion from just those quarters. What happened next? One by one I watched my acquaintances, openly or surreptitiously according to their natures, join a westward migration, some to south-western England, many more to Wales. Irresistibly caught up, my small son and I found ourselves in Dorset, a unit in this mass movement to the west. How reminiscent it was of an earlier Germanic onslaught, when the warlike and pagan Anglo-Saxons swept down on eastern Britain and unhappy Celts fled before them to seek safety among the western hills!

As the summer of 1940 advanced, Germanic hordes were reported to be massing down the French coast, and the whole of southern England became uneasy. This again followed the prehistoric pattern, for throughout the Stone, Bronze and Iron Ages our southern shores had been invaded from France. In our particular western corner of Dorset we talked of the unpleasant proximity of Normandy and Brittany: of boats rumoured to be gathering at Cherbourg and Brest. I reminded myself how Dorset had received invaders from Brittany in Neolithic times, at the beginning of the Bronze Age, and again in the Iron Age.

Then Italy. Letters from friends in Cornwall hinted that the Italians might threaten their security; others held that Ireland would be the victim. Here again prehistory could show analogies, for archaeology has proved that those areas were always accessible to movements springing from the Mediterranean, for instance, that which brought the megalithic chieftains 4000 years ago.

There could have been nothing unexpected in such repetition of the past. Whatever may be true in the future, it is clear that at that time not even aeroplanes had altered the control that geography exercises over human movements.

But now it has all grown distant and unreal, quite as far from recall as the events of prehistory; I find it hard to believe that this body of mine took part in the great exodus from Paddington, that it had a place in the trains crowded with migrating families – these things might have happened at any time. Faint and impersonal though the memory now is, this opening digression has been allowed in order to give some idea of the natural routes by which settlers and conquerors have at all times approached the British Isles. Chapter I will immediately follow with some account of the nature of the country itself.

PREHISTORIC BRITAIN

The Palaeolithic and Mesolithic Ages

To all except the most urbanized among us the physical nature of our country is of profound significance. The widely differing types of scenery that Britain can offer in so small a space have entered our consciousness at an early age, beginning perhaps with the first summer holidays that took us out of a familiar scene and into a strange one. No need for knowledge of geological formations to be aware of their powerful influence on the countryside they nourish. There is an instinctive appreciation of the difference between the dry, golden feeling of the sandy heaths, the pale, clear atmosphere of the chalk, the boundless, open-skyed freedom of fenlands, and the damp chill that strikes up from the heavy clay soil of the Midlands. They appeal to different temperaments and different moods. Yet, distinctive though these several kinds of country are, they have something in common, for all belong to the lowlands of southern, central and eastern England: an even greater contrast is to be found between these lowlands as a whole and the highlands of the west and north. Geologically the lowlands are young, and have the soft contours of youth, while the ancient rocks forming the highlands show the rugged features of a strong old age.

The line dividing these two worlds runs from east Devon to the southern boundary of Durham, but the highland zone is broken between the northern Welsh mountains and the

Pennine Chain by the intrusion of the Midland Gap and the Cheshire Plain. North and west of that line one cannot be the same man that breathes south and east of it; the mountains, moorlands, swift streams, bogs, and their attendant trees, plants, birds and fishes work a transformation. Crossing it means more than crossing the Channel, for the highland zone is far more alien to the lowland than the latter is to the adjacent parts of northern France and Flanders.

If to-day we are still acutely conscious of these divisions within our country, early man had to be much more so. Centuries of cultivation have minimized the distinctions between the various regions of the lowland zone, while modern transport hurries one without effort across boundaries that were once formidable. On Shanks' mare in a roadless land the traveller had a very different outlook. When man's ordering of the natural scene was unthought of or only just begun, he could not fail to be ever aware of the environment that was his master. What were the main geographical factors that limited prehistoric man's choice of movement and settlement? For the moment it is best to leave behind those more remote ages when Britain formed an unrecognizable part of the Continent, and deal only with the time when it had assumed approximately its present shape and temperate climate.

Consider first the forests. In prehistoric times no considerable progress was made in clearing the dense covering of oakwood and thorny undergrowth supported by the heavier and richer soils. This luxuriant growth, and the damp soil beneath, made great tracts of the lowlands, including much of the Midlands, impossible for human settlement and all but impenetrable.

In the days before drainage, marshland, too, was much more extensive; the East Anglian fens and the Vale of York formed the largest water-logged areas, but very many valley bottoms now pleasantly lined with green meadows were then swampy and hard to traverse.

It was only where soil was light and pervious, poor regions in the eyes of the modern farmer, that men were able to clear and settle the land. Hence the overwhelming concentration of prehistoric sites on chalk and limestone uplands, sandy soil, and the gravel of some valleys. For many people the great monuments of Stonehenge and Avebury, with the barrows and other satellites clustering round them, represent the essential core of all British antiquity. There is sound reason in this belief, however emotional its inspiration. The region in which they stand was all-important owing to its commanding geographical position. The physical map shows clearly how the Wiltshire Downlands form the nodal point of the lands suitable for prehistoric occupation. Not only does the chalk here reach its widest extent, but from it radiate all the principal chalk and limestone ranges of lowland Britain: the Mendips point towards the Bristol Channel; the Western Downs stretch far into Dorset; the Hampshire Downs, forking into the North and South Downs, reach the English Channel in Kent and Sussex; the Chiltern Hills linking with the East Anglian Heights penetrate to the North Sea; and finally the Cotswolds and Northampton Uplands finger northwards and make contact possible with the wide, habitable region of the Lincolnshire and Yorkshire Wolds. Equally important, the Wiltshire Downs are accessible by navigable rivers, most significantly by the Thames, which early formed a vital thoroughfare and whose gravel-filled valley was always favourable to settlement. Thus the whole of this wheel-like system had a kind of unity, and on its uplands men could rear their flocks and herds, their children and their crops, looking down on the forests that pushed

17

up between the spokes, formidable and hostile, the haunt of bears, wolves, lynx, and perhaps of evil spirits.

Very different problems confronted would-be settlers in the highland country. There the upland ranges were shunned as boggy, windswept and generally inhospitable, the valley bottoms were blocked by oak forest, while then as now the extreme acidity of highland soil discouraged agriculture. Their choice was thus mainly limited to coastal belts such as that of eastern Scotland, where glaciers had left a more profitable soil, and to narrow coastal glens, peninsulas, and islands where well-drained ground was offered by the remains of old sea beaches. They could also take possession of the flanks of mountain valleys lying between the forested bottoms and the bleak crests above. There are signs that man could not afford entirely to ignore the high moorlands: probably he visited them during the summer when they could provide fair grazing for his beasts. Indeed, in the kinder climate of the south-west, uplands such as Dartmoor and Exmoor could be permanently settled and were at times quite populous.

Another strong contrast with the lowlands. While there we have found a general accessibility between all the habitable territories, in the mountainous country, especially in western Scotland and Wales, each little settled area tended to be cut off from the next by almost impassable barriers. To some extent, however, the prehistoric communities escaped the isolation that their land would have imposed by launching boats and finding easier and swifter passage by sea than any mountain trail could allow. Nor did their craft always hug the shore: there was often free intercourse across the Irish Sea between south-west Scotland, north Wales, the Isle of Man and Ulster. If Ireland falls outside our main survey, she can never be forgotten. Inevitably her fate was closely linked

with that of the British highlands that reached out towards
her even while they walled her off from England and the
Continent.

These, then, were the two great zones of Britain with their
contrasting pattern of human settlement. What was the
relationship between them: the reaction of one upon the
other? Modern analogy has been used to show how the lowlands were always prone to invasion from the opposing continental shores, and how each wave of immigrants tended to
push some of the older population into the hills. The new
impulse might well itself reach the highlands, but attenuated
and transfigured. Once there it would be further modified
alike by a strong conservative tradition and by fresh external
influences. For the highlands had their own contact with the
Continent along the Atlantic sea routes from Brittany to
Portugal, and thence with the Mediterranean both by sea
round the coast of the Iberian Peninsula and by land across
its neck. They also had an all-important asset in their possession of metal ores: gold in Ireland, tin in Cornwall, and
copper in Ireland, Cornwall, north Wales and western Scotland. Thus the highlands had distinctive ingredients to add
to the British stock-pot.

The curious, intricate outline of these islands perched on
the edge of Europe has from childhood become so strongly
engraved on our minds that it seems to have something of
unalterable truth. In fact, of course, the British Isles are
infinitely younger than man. Human beings of a kind have
inhabited our world for at least half a million years: the
chalk hills that stretched across the present line of the English
Channel were not finally breached until quite recently, some
eight thousand years ago, while much of the North Sea was
still land at an even later date.

The map of Britain began to assume its present form

during the last great geological epoch, that of the Pleistocene, which covers the period often called the Ice Age. This name is misleading, for it suggests an age of continuous cold, whereas in fact it was divided into distinct cold phases, probably at least four in number, with intervals when the European climate was sometimes much warmer than at present.

At the height of the cold conditions Scotland and a great part of England lay under vast ice-sheets and glaciers: the intervening spells saw the retreat of the ice towards the north and the spread of warmth-loving plants and animals in its wake. These glaciations remodelled the face of Britain. They caused changes in sea-level, the land standing sometimes higher and sometimes lower than to-day. Thus old land surfaces could become sea floors, and the deposits then formed on them re-emerge into the air as new land, while former shorelines might be left high and dry, sometimes far inland. Melting glaciers combined with these changes in level to re-shape river valleys, filling them with gravel and channelling it into stepped terraces. The ice itself exercised tremendous power. It cut and moulded the northern mountains and valleys, and farther south laid down beneath it and around its edges the accumulated material torn up and pulverized during its slow journeying. In this way was formed the boulder clay which covers so much of the Midlands; outwash from the glaciers could also spread wide expanses of plateau gravels, and far beyond the actual extent of the ice, soil formation was affected by the freezing and thawing of winter and summer. When the sheet-ice and the glaciers had finally dispersed, these deposits remained to transform the countryside, control its future vegetation, and thus ultimately do much to dictate the lines of its human settlement.

When did creatures recognizably human first begin to play

their part against this geological background? It is a hard question because recognition is itself so uncertain. In the long line of ape-like figures, which shall we select as the first of our human ancestors? Perhaps it is best so to distinguish the first creature to shape a tool. For the ability to do so is exclusively human – apes may use implements but never fashion them. They were man's substitute for the specialized horns, fangs and hoofs evolved by the beasts; although less efficient at first, they were to conquer in the end through their greater adaptability. Certainly tool-making is a more expedient criterion for the prehistorian to employ than bodily characteristics, for implements when made of stone will survive while almost all skeletal material perishes.

The idea of creating any tool artificially was entirely new – such a thing had never before happened in the world: naturally the earliest attempts would be very crude, and therefore difficult to identify. That is the position of eoliths. This name has been given to certain types of chipped flints that were first discovered in the plateau gravels on the North Downs of Kent, where geology may assign them to the Tertiary period, well before the beginning of the Ice Age. There is, however, nothing to show if the chipping is artificial or merely the product of natural forces – it does not follow any of the rules of later human workmanship.

It will probably always be disputed whether these eoliths do in fact represent the first fumbling attempts of man to arm for the infinitely long struggle between Nature and himself which stretched into the future over thousands of generations. But with the scene set for the Ice Age man steps well on to the stage and begins the play in which we ourselves are acting.

The phase of human history corresponding to the Pleistocene or Ice Age of geological time is known as the Palaeolithic or Old Stone Age. It was at least a thousand times longer than the time that has elapsed since the Biblical Flood, yet the material progress achieved by Palaeolithic man was slight indeed when compared with that made by the descendants of Noah. But there was progress: slowly as he learnt more of the character of the natural resources available, he improved his equipment, shaped his tools more skilfully, and adapted them to increasingly specialized tasks. Very early, too, he learnt to make use of one of Nature's most dramatic chemical processess – fire. Behind and impelling this process of material improvement was an all-important mental growth, which was to find an outlet in coherent speech. Speech, springing from the most rudimentary beginnings, became a vehicle for carrying the fruits of experience from generation to generation. As words became more numerous, sensitive and abstract, man's intellectual conceptions could grow more complex; it is difficult for us to follow them through the medium of stones and bones, but we get a glimpse when we find him furnishing the dead with tools and food as though anticipating an after-life, and they are more fully revealed by the end of the age, when he had become master of a highly accomplished art with a magical content.

Our contacts with the earliest Palaeolithic men are confined to stone tools found incorporated in geological deposits and the rare discovery of actual skeletal remains; it is only later that a rather more complete and intimate picture can be drawn from the contents of cave dwellings. The earliest phases have been most successfully studied in the rich Pleistocene deposits that survive in East Anglia. These suggest that men were already shaping flints there well before the first onset of the ice, but it is not until the ensuing warmer interval that the evidence is unambiguous. But already by then two quite distinct methods of tool-making had been

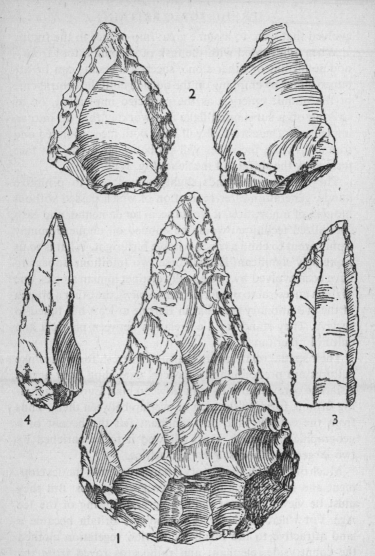

FIG. 1. Flint implements of the Palaeolithic Age.

evolved that were to assume great importance in the future.

When confronted with the task of shaping a tool from a nodule of flint or other stone, successful results can be obtained either by chipping off the outside until the central core of the nodule emerges as the perfected implement, or by striking off a substantial flake and working that up into an implement. The core-tool will have both faces rounded and trimmed, while the other will probably have one flat face formed by the surface of the flake (Fig. 1, no. 2).

The distinction sounds slight enough, yet to primitive minds, generation after generation of which passed without thought of innovation, it would seem fundamental, and each specialized technique would be handed on unquestioningly from parent to child as an inevitable birthright. What is to us supremely significant is that these two traditions appear to have been evolved by two equally distinct human stocks, one of them ancestral to modern *Homo sapiens*, the other a branch of the evolutionary tree that in Europe at least has failed to survive. They stand for a correlation between physical and cultural inheritance.

Their spatial relationship is also of interest, for while flake cultures are predominantly Eastern, extending right across Asia, the core cultures have an African bias: Europe, including Britain, forming the area of overlap between them. Thus from the earliest time our continent felt the benefit of a geographical position which allowed it to be enriched by two larger neighbours, Asia and Africa.

Much of Palaeolithic history is concerned with the development and interactions of these two great groups. But they must be viewed against the ebbing and flowing of the Ice Age. For when the sun was triumphant Britain became a land attractive to life of all kinds, rich vegetation clothed the countryside, elephant and rhinoceros roved from the

Thames valley to East Anglia, hippopotami floated in the rivers and wallowed in the swamps; when the ice had the victory, southern England alone remained habitable, and there vegetation was reduced to a low scrub, rivers froze and valleys were blocked with snow for many months: only such hardy animals as mammoth, bison and reindeer could endure even the summer weather. And just as the big creatures replaced one another, so did the infinitely small: everywhere among leaves and grasses, in ponds and rivers, a host of tiny species were gradually superseded by others as the temperature changed, leaving their shells to record their fate, and therewith climatic history. Man also had to submit, almost as helplessly, for his elementary material equipment had as yet hardly begun to give him independence of his environment. The core-culture folk at the height of the cold phases seem, like the warmth-loving animals, to have retreated southward towards Africa, returning again with the milder weather. The flake peoples, on the other hand, with their more robust bodies and – one dare guess – hairier skins, may have been able to survive much closer to the edge of the ice. Each tradition shows its own cultural developments, and these have been named after sites where they are well represented – too often for the ease of our English tongues the chosen sites are French. The core culture which flourished during the first interglacial phase is the Abbevillian, already characterized by an implement always to remain the principal core form, a heavy, pear-shaped, all-purpose tool, rather meaninglessly known to archaeology as the hand-axe (Fig. 1, no. 1). By the time England again became habitable this culture had been greatly improved into the Acheulian, whose hand-axes were more shapely, had sharper cutting edges, and owed their smoother finish to a new method of flaking with a wooden or bone bar in place of the hammer-stone. The

Acheulian lasted through the greater part of Palaeolithic times, the hand-axe tending to grow lighter and more elegant and the subsidary tools more varied. It should be borne in mind that our area forms only a very small province of the Acheulian culture, for during the immensely long life it enjoyed its bearers were able to spread all over western and southern Europe, Africa, Palestine, and most of India.

Meanwhile the flake tradition also had its innovations: every ten thousand years or so it might produce a genius with a new idea for cultural improvement or change. Contemporary with the earliest Abbevillian, apparently, there was a flake culture, which rather before the return of the Acheulians, after the second cold phase, had given rise to the Clactonian. This was a culture which in time could show excellent flint work, largely in the form of pointed and sharp-edged tools made on heavy flakes and intended for all kinds of cutting and scraping, including the dressing of animal skins. To the Clactonian and Acheulian traditions was presently added the Levalloisian; this became outstanding during the last interglacial, when it was responsible for beautifully finished points and scrapers which, by an ingenious new technique, were partially trimmed before the flake was struck from the parent core.

Abbevillian, Acheulian, Clactonian, Levalloisian, what do these ponderous names, based on their flinty foundations, represent in terms of human living? The economics of a very primitive food-gathering life must have demanded a small mobile group, probably united by ties of kinship (and, if we may believe Freud, already riddled with the Oedipus complex). The men would have hunted game, while the women and children gathered everything that experience had taught them was edible of fruits, roots and grubs. Probably when the climate was warm their diet would have been predominantly vegetarian: one can imagine how a week's gorging on elephant flesh might be followed by a long period when no meat was to be had. In hunting the larger animals men must have used their cunning and ability for co-operative effort to devise traps and organize drives.

As to the personal appearance of these early hunters, we know nothing of what is usually implied by these words – hair, eyes and complexion can be supplied only by the imagination – but we have some valuable scraps of evidence as to the bony structure which they covered. No remains likely to belong to a flake-tool maker have been found in this country, but we can turn to a contemporary who left a lower jaw to be incorporated in the Mauer sands near Heidelberg in Germany. This being must have been powerfully built and ape-like, for the jaw is chinless, but very heavy and armed with extraordinarily massive teeth. A vitally important discovery made in England allows us to form a rather more certain idea of the core culture people. Patient watching of the quarries that are gradually biting into the mass of gravel laid down by the Pleistocene Thames had for many years yielded only animal bones and flints, but at last in 1935 part of a human skull came as a sudden reward. Its position in the Barnfield Pit at Swanscombe in association with fine hand-axes allows it to be recognized as the only quite certain representative of Acheulian man known to the world. The measurement of the two bones was followed with intense interest, which was heightened when it appeared how closely they resemble those of modern man. The Swanscombe skull, indeed, provides some of the best evidence for attributing the hand-axe cultures to our own direct ancestors.

The famous Piltdown Man of Sussex was long held to be at least equally ancient, but newly developed methods of dating by chemical analysis have shown almost beyond question that this skull is less than one hundred thousand years old. Piltdown Man had a well developed forehead and cranial vault not unlike those of modern man, although the bone is of exceptional thickness; his jaw, on the other hand (and the analysis suggests that it belonged to the same individual, a fact which had been doubted), is apelike both in its chinlessness and in the formation of some of the teeth. It seems that this species of man must represent an offshoot from the human stem which was to prove unsuccessful, but which survived for a very long time before becoming extinct.

In the earlier Palaeolithic ages which we have been considering, the core and the flake traditions seem to have held aloof, each pursuing its own line of development; but in time they began to react upon each other, and in the third and last interglacial it seems that the Acheulian, Clactonian and Levalloisian traditions actually borrowed techniques and tool-forms from one another. How far this implies also close social contacts between the two stocks is quite unknown, but it is not impossible to believe that they interbred.

One of the products of the stimulating interaction between the older traditions was a new flake culture, the Mousterian, which enjoyed its heyday during the final glaciation of the Ice Age. It is a familiar name owing to its association with Neanderthal man, that last descendant of the flake-tool makers whose very lack of charm seems to have made him the most popular of prehistoric figures. Everyone has read of his beetling brows, his prominent teeth, his chinlessness, his hairiness, and has seen them reproduced in pictures, even in bronze busts. There is an appeal in this ape-like being who yet had the skill of a man and some of his sentiments. His tools show excellent workmanship, and he has provided the earliest known instances of the careful burial and equipping of the dead.

The last cold phase was less intense than its predecessor and was broken up by slightly milder interludes. Nevertheless living must have been harsh enough in the tundra conditions prevailing beyond the limits of the ice, and although the tough Neanderthal physique was well adapted to endure them, it is not surprising that shelter against the worst rigours of winter was sought in caves. In Britain two were certainly inhabited at this time – Kent's Cavern near Torquay, and the Pin Hole in the Derbyshire limestone ravine of Creswell Crags – the oldest recognizable human dwellings in our country.

While Neanderthal man with his Mousterian flake culture was dominant in an ice-bound continent, where were the descendants of Swanscombe man? Were any still living in western Europe? This is an unsolved problem. The Mousterian often shows borrowings from Acheulian as well as Levalloisian sources, and therefore, although none of their skeletons is known, it is not inconceivable that some descendants of the hand-axe people may have maintained themselves side by side with their more simian contemporaries. However this may be, late glacial times saw the complete triumph of our ancestral stock. With what now seems dramatic suddenness the beings whose appearance in a modern street would probably lead to their exhibition in Regent's Park were displaced by men who, if suitably clad, would hardly cause a stir at the Athenaeum, still less at the Savage. In fact, of course, this dispossession must have been spread over many generations, but it is certainly true that everywhere in Europe the Mousterian and parallel flake cultures vanish completely, together with all traces of Neanderthal Man, while his caves and hunting-grounds were taken over by men of modern type with a very different material culture. With the arrogance bred of our survival, it is very easy for us to see the Neanderthalers as low, brutish and altogether unworthy of continuance on this earth; but if history had gone otherwise, perhaps if the weather had been rather different, how readily they would have dismissed *Homo sapiens* as a highbrow weakling fully deserving his extinction!

The late Palaeolithic hunters had a much more delicate and specialized equipment than their predecessors, that is distinguished from the core and flake forms by the general name of 'blade' culture (Fig. 1, nos. 3 and 4). Their flint implements, all much smaller and lighter than anything usual before, were often made on narrow, parallel-sided flakes and blades, which enabled them to find the tradition of the cutting knife which has remained an essential human tool ever since. In addition, these people made flint chisels which helped them to master a new technique, the carving of bone, and in time to produce beautifully finished and elaborate forms such as multi-barbed harpoons and spear-throwers in this medium. The spear-thrower has a special significance. It is the first known instance of the use of a mechanical principle, that of the lever, for supplementing mere man-power. *Homo sapiens* had already started on that career of mechanic which has him in its grip to-day.

Another important accomplishment for which the earliest evidence dates from this period is the making of fire; man had made use of it from very early times, but now he knew how to create it for himself by striking flint against a natural metallic substance, such as iron pyrites. In the bitter weather wandering hunting-parties must have been saved many hardships and dangers by their ability to light camp-fires against the cold, darkness and beasts of the night.

These great advances in man's armament against Nature enabled him to take full advantage of the ideal hunting conditions offered in late glacial Europe, where mammoth, reindeer, woolly rhinoceros, bison and horse throve on the steppe and tundra. In particularly favoured regions, such as south-west France and northern Spain, food supplies were now so easily obtained that the hunters had the economic security and leisure necessary to enable them for the first time to realize some of the spiritual potentialities of their humanity. Ritual, centred on hunting-magic and fertility cults, must have played a vital part in their lives, and to serve it they built up artistic schools that produced animal paintings, engravings and carvings hardly to be surpassed in their inspired naturalism. A desire and veneration for fertility seem to have found expression in statuettes of pregnant women that often show a wonderful control of form in their full, voluptuous lines. It is one of the most astonishing events in human history that in this, its first liberation, man's artistic impulse should have created works that still, after tens of thousands of years, convey genuine aesthetic pleasure, and which can be judged without condescension by any modern standards (Fig. 2).

But these spiritual achievements were confined to the centres materially best endowed: that part of western Europe destined to become the British Isles was too remote, too ice-ridden, to support so high a standard of life. Probably the population never amounted to more than a few hundred souls, mainly absorbed in the quest for food. Caves in Derbyshire, north and south Wales, the Wye valley and the Mendips were occupied, but the majority only sporadically and for short periods; artistic content is extremely rare, and even flint and bone tools are generally poor and scanty.

In France an elaborate sequence of late Palaeolithic blade cultures has been recognized, some introduced from farther east, some developed locally, but not all of them penetrated to our region. The first to do so was the Aurignacian, a

Fig. 2. Palaeolithic Cave paintings in France and Spain.

culture originating in the Near East and spreading across Europe finally to reach Britain as a western outpost. The Aurignacians included skilled hunters and artists, and were excellent technicians in flint, trimming their tools with long, narrow flakes that gave an elegant fluted effect.

The next stray bands to arrive were Gravettians, a people with a rather more northerly range than their predecessors, who in south Russia and elsewhere had used their human wits to prey successfully upon the formidable mammoth herds and build up a way of life that was largely parasitic on these great creatures. A long occupation of the Pin Hole Cave allows us to watch the gradual evolution of the culture into a form sufficiently distinct to warrant a name of its own, the Creswellian. This can be saluted as the first specifically British culture, poor cousin though it is to its brilliantly successful French counterpart, the Magdalenian, which saw Palaeolithic skill and artistry reach their highest perfection. A few examples of the fine Magdalenian bone-work have been found in this country, as far south as Kent's Cavern and as far north as the West Riding, but we cannot guess if these were brought by actual immigrants driven by circumstance from their own more congenial territories, or whether, as valuable and sought-after objects, they had been bartered from hand to hand.

The many skeletons unearthed from European caves (a corpse in the home did not trouble and may even have encouraged these people) give a fair idea of the racial types of the men responsible for the late Palaeolithic blade cultures. Already they were varied, but clear correlation cannot always be established between racial and cultural divisions. There were powerful and slight physiques, long and short faces, while round skulls existed side by side with the dominant long-head form.

PB–2

Most of the late Palaeolithic inhabitants of Britain belonged to the Crô-Magnon race, tall, robust men with round but strongly boned faces, and usually, though not invariably, long-headed. Their most famous representative is the Red Lady of Paviland who was excavated in South Wales by the great Dr Buckland early in the nineteenth century. This discovery should have won prominence as the first of a Palaeolithic cave burial, but Buckland was destined to become a Dean as well as a professor of geology, and his theologian's conscience, mindful of the creation of man in 4004 B.C., obliged him to dissociate the human bones from those of the extinct animals among which they lay, and attribute them to a lady living at about the time of the Roman Conquest. His choice of names was no happier than his chronology, for the Red Lady was in fact a young man who had been ceremonially buried, together with his personal ornaments and an elephant's head, under a covering of red ochre. The use of this substance, known also on the Continent, gives a hint of the mentality of those responsible, for they may have conceived that its redness gave to ochre the life-giving power of blood.

The wealthy hunting societies of late glacial Europe might have maintained or even enriched their culture, or allowed it to stagnate and decline: they could hardly have advanced to a higher form of civilization, for the environment forbade it. But their future was not left in their own hands. Inexorably, although no doubt to them imperceptibly, the climate changed: summers grew longer and warmer, ice-sheets shrank and glaciers retreated. Enslaved to climate, plant and animal life had to change also. The mammoth, rhinoceros and reindeer in turn disappeared from western Europe, their going perhaps accelerated by the inroads of the human hunters themselves. On what had been open grassland or tundra with a scrub of dwarf birch and willow, forests spread, stocked with the appropriate forest animals – red deer, aurochs and wild pig. With the withdrawal or extinction of the great herds on which they had preyed, the economic basis of the hunting societies was cut away and their carefully adjusted culture made obsolete. This was one of the moments when early man was able to prove the full advantage of his self-made equipment over the biological specialization of the beasts: the reindeer found his coat intolerably hot and had to quit, man merely took his off and readjusted his habits.

The results of his labours were the Mesolithic cultures. These show two main trends in the adaptation of tool forms. One, already manifest in late Palaeolithic developments such as the Creswellian, was the reduction of the size of flints to a 'microlithic' scale, accompanied no doubt by a freer use of the now abundant wood for hafting them, several together, as composite tools. This represented little more than a compromise between the old Palaeolithic ideas and new needs. The other was the inventing of heavy wood-cutting tools to deal with that fresh factor and problem of the day, the forest. Armed with these axes, colonists were able to settle regions of northern Europe that had exchanged a covering of ice for one of trees, and there establish Forest cultures well adjusted to the changed conditions.

If these Mesolithic adaptations show no advance on Palaeolithic cultural standards, but indeed in many ways, as in the loss of art, a sad decline, they did at least allow the old human stocks to survive in Europe and conserve a physical and material contribution for the future civilization that was to reach our continent from without.

Britain received three streams of Mesolithic immigration: the Forest culture known as the Maglemosian from the east, and two of the more purely microlithic cultures, the

Tardenoisian and the Azilian, from the south and south-west. They were the first to follow the three lines of approach to this country whose use, as we have seen, was to become habitual.

The newcomers must have found already in possession a poor indigenous population descended from the late Palaeolithic Creswellians. Indeed, these natives long contrived to maintain their independence, some of them migrating to Ireland thousands of years later.

The Maglemosians probably crossed the area now covered by the North Sea as fishers and fowlers, working their way over mere-studded fens, making use of dug-out canoes steered

FIG. 3. Mesolithic bone prong from the North Sea.

and propelled with broad-bladed wooden paddles. Such a canoe was found below the clays laid down by the river Tay at Perth, which allows Scotland to claim the oldest known boat in western Europe. On the way one of their number lost a precious bone prong from his fish-spear, which was only recovered some 10,000 years later, in 1931, when another fisherman found it in his net, trawled up from over 20 fathoms not many miles off the Norfolk coast (Fig. 3).

Once they reached the slightly higher ground that was soon to become the east coast of the British Isles, the Maglemosians occupied the river valleys and low plains suited to their means of subsistence. The men must have hunted game and small fur-bearing animals, gone fowling for duck, geese, cranes, and many other birds, and fished extensively with pronged spears, barbless bone hooks and nets. The women's contribution of vegetable foods was augmented by the spread of trees and shrubs – hazel nuts in particular were relished – and they also would have been responsible for collecting the shell-fish that became an increasingly important element in the Mesolithic diet.

The Forest folk's great contribution to the material culture of the age, their wood-cutting tools, were at first best represented by heavy core axes, but later an improved form made on a flake, and with a wide cutting edge, largely displaced them. These tools would have been used alike for felling timber and for such carpenter's jobs as hollowing out canoes and shaping paddles.

In short, the Maglemosians enjoyed a life tolerably well provided with material comfort, at least in the summer, but they did nothing to maintain the Palaeolithic artistic traditions. Whether this was due to lack of economic plenty, and hence of leisure, or to a lack of genius, or the usual complicated balance between the two, we shall never know: perhaps it was due to fear of representational magic.

In comparison with these Forest people the Tardenoisians are shadowy figures. Their microlithic culture originated perhaps in north Africa, whence it was obliged to expand by the increasing desiccation which there followed the end of the Ice Age. They carried it over a wide area of western Europe, probably reaching Britain from north France and Belgium. We know them almost entirely from finds of their tiny flints made on the sandy lands to which their lack of wood-cutting tools restricted them. They were also able to make summer excursions to open uplands such as the Pennines, where a number of temporary camping sites furnished with rough hearths have been preserved below the peat beds. They were a neat-fingered people, for their microliths, although often measuring no more than half an inch long, are yet meticulously trimmed – one group of them into precise geometric shapes. The majority of these pygmy flints they must have set in wooden shafts to make arrows, darts and spears for hunting the small game and birds to their sandy territories. Dogs are now for the first time found attached to human settlements and were presumably used in the chase. The Tardenoisians can therefore claim to have originated the institution of the canine friend that has survived to become one of the most cherished and most hated of our national foibles.

The Azilians, who brought from the south of France a microlithic culture of Magdalenian descent no better adapted than the Tardenoisian to cope with forest conditions, found a different means of avoiding them in settling as strand-loopers along the coastal fringe. They were successful sea-fishermen, collected shell-fish, nuts and probably sea-birds' eggs, went fowling, and hunted deer, boar and smaller animals. The best known of their settlements are all in south-west Scotland, two cave shelters near Oban, and a camping site on the island of Oronsay, but others must have existed along the shores of Wales and south-west England that have since been submerged by the sea. The debt of their culture to the Magdalenian is particularly evident in their most characteristic implement, a flat, rather feebly barbed bone harpoon which is clearly a degeneration from the elegant Palaeolithic form.

Once established in Britain, these Mesolithic cultures began to influence one another and give rise to original insular developments. One of them was that of the Horsham people who used pygmy tools like those of the Tardenoisians, but had also adopted heavy axes in the Maglemosian tradition. They it was who have left us some of the oldest artificial dwellings known in this country: a little settlement clustered round the source of a spring at Farnham in Surrey. For shelter they had scooped the floors of their irregularly shaped huts well into the ground, roofing them with boughs and perhaps with sods.

The term insular which has just been applied to these developments of late Mesolithic times can now for the first time be justly employed. It was almost certainly during the Mesolithic period, and possibly about 6000 B.C., that England became separated from the Continent. Over the fenny country traversed by the early Maglemosians swept a rising North Sea. It is fitting that already in the opening phase of Britain's isolation we can watch this blending of cultures of diverse origin and their assumption of an unmistakable local character; it was a process often to be repeated during her future history. For Britain now acquired the peculiar powers of an island. Just as among the Galapagos Darwin found that island birds evolved a special plumage, we shall see that after crossing the Channel continental cultures assume a distinctively British colouring. Yet she escaped the peculiar danger of an island – stagnation through lack of stimulus. Her exposed lowlands were always sufficiently near and hospitable to invite across the water both colonists and traders.

Before the end of Mesolithic times changes in climate followed, and were perhaps partly caused by, these changes in sea-level. Since the end of the Ice Age Britain had enjoyed a climate of the 'continental' type – dry and with warm summers – but now the weather grew much wetter, south-west winds bringing rain and mist from the Atlantic. The increasing moisture modified the nature of the forests, driving out the pines that had dominated them in early post-glacial days; instead damp oak woods with abundant alder occupied all the heavy soils, and Britain assumed the complexion described at the beginning of this chapter, which must have lasted with no further essential change throughout the rest of prehistoric times.

The end of an epoch was at hand. During the immense span of time since the birth of our first tool-making human, man had lived by taking the animals, fruits and plants which Nature spread before him on the face of the earth. Certainly he had grown more successful, acquiring a store of knowledge and skill built up through thousands of years of bitter experience. Yet he still lived very much as the fowls of the air. He had not thought either to sow or to reap. The time for this was coming, and with it infinite possibilities for human enrichment.

Any modern visitor to Mesolithic Britain would hardly be able to guess that anything so momentous was astir. He would see poor little groups of hunters and food-gatherers scattered round the fringes and in the clearings of the dripping forests. And watching the Azilian woman crouching among the rocks as she dislodges limpets with a stone, the Tardenoisian with his flint-tipped arrow lying in wait for a hare, or even the Maglemosian leaning over the prow of his canoe with a glistening fish thrashing between the prongs of his spear, he would not think that the foundations of his civilization were being laid. Nor were they by these people, or in this country, or indeed in Europe. It was in the East that new and propitious combinations of sun, soil, water, seeds and animal life were suggesting to men the possibility for revolutionary change.

CHAPTER II

The Neolithic Age

THE hunting life may be a good one: dangerous, certainly, but full of excitement and free from the monotony of routine existence. Given ideal conditions it may be so easy and leisurely that it allows men time and freedom of spirit to adorn it with the joys of art and ritual. But the story already told of the catastrophic collapse of the Palaeolithic hunting civilization caused by the changing climate at the end of the Ice Age illustrates its greatest weakness: the insecurity inherent in complete dependence on natural food supplies. When the spread of forests in western Europe deprived the great herds of their livelihood, and their disappearance in turn robbed man of his, he could save himself only by the adaptability that has always been his greatest strength. We have seen how the Mesolithic cultures, with their lowered standard of living, were the best answer he could make to this challenge. But the very different problems that were posed by the contemporary changes of climate in the East provoked a totally different response. It will never be known what part individual genius and initiative played in seizing the opportunities that were offered, but the outcome is well known: man began to escape his complete subservience to his surroundings, and instead to make nature serve his own purposes.

Centres existed in the Middle East where animals and plants suitable for domestication by man flourished in conditions that prompted him to attempt it. The shifting of rainbelts across the world at the end of the Ice Age meant that while in western Europe the open grazing-grounds became wet and tree-ridden, in these more southerly zones they became, little by little, desiccated and desert. This withering of their food supply forced the animals to herd hungrily round the scattered oases, and there they would come into contact with human settlement. Thus it was natural enough that man should have the idea of exercising some control over the habits and movements of the herds that he daily saw about him. At first, no doubt, his authority was slight and his flocks lived in as nearly wild a state as the reindeer of the modern Lapp, but as the animals themselves grew more docile it increased, until with the practice of careful selective breeding man had gone far in his interference with nature.

If it was the hunting male who is likely to have been responsible for the domestication of animals, woman should probably be credited with the great parallel advance of this time – the cultivation of plants. It had always fallen to her to gather the wild vegetable foods, and when she had watched some forgotten handful of seeds sprout into new life, the notion of deliberate sowing might readily suggest itself. Here again selective propagation would in time improve the wild strains, and, granted sufficient rainfall, greatly increase their yield. We do not know which plants were the first to be cultivated, but cereals, and particularly wheat, certainly came to be the most important.

To all of us arable and pasture fields and grazing beasts are so familiar and essential a part of the countryside that it is hard to picture a world in which none such existed. Indeed, many of us go farther, and see the regular arrival of the wheaten loaf and the milk-bottle as belonging to the natural order of things. It is correspondingly difficult to think ourselves back into the lives of those who initiated the revolution that has ended in our baker's loaves and bottled milk.

How would the adoption of stock-breeding and agriculture affect human living and its material progress? Obviously, while pastoralism would allow and in some circumstances encourage a degree of nomadism, mixed farming with agriculture would demand a much more settled way of life that was likely to lead to the establishment of village communities and an organized society. Perhaps this development affected the lives of women even more than of men: they could put down their babies in safety and have their hands and minds free to follow the practical creative bent that has always brought their greatest satisfaction. And the new type of life gave fresh scope to inventiveness. The product of their liberated genius was the many domestic crafts, such as potting, weaving and fine basketry, which in simple societies they have continued to practise ever since.

This first great acceleration in material progress has been called the Neolithic Revolution, and it unquestionably had a deeper effect on the everyday life of men and women than any other episode in human history before the Industrial Revolution of the last centuries. And what an astounding acceleration it was! As far as we can judge, all the advances described – the invention of mixed farming and the new crafts – culminated within a single millennium, somewhere between 6000 and 5000 B.C. – a very brief span when set against the vast, uneventful stretches of Palaeolithic time.

In the Middle East, where it began, this rapid progress was long hurried on by its own momentum. The surplus food which the new methods yielded beyond the mere subsistence of its producers not only caused a big rise in population, but made possible the support by society of increasingly skilled specialists in more and more numerous crafts. And to supply them with the needful materials a trading class was born to hunt the Near East and the Mediterranean for such rare and magical substances as malachite and obsidian and lapis lazuli, until, in time, the search was extended to metals. The discovery of the properties of copper, and then of its alloy with tin, bronze, had far-reaching economic, social and intellectual results. The ores were never obtainable in the early centres of civilization, but had to be searched out in remote mountains and carried long distances, and in response to such demands for transport came the invention of the wheeled cart and the sailing-ship. A host of new processes, many of them involving complicated chemical change, had to be devised and mastered – smelting, alloying, hammering and casting; in fact, man was becoming a scientist, however empirical his methods.

All these activities could not be conducted from the simple villages of the old Neolithic communities; the mutual interests of the specialists drew them together and urban life began – cities grew up as centres of manufacture and commerce. Nor did the surplus wealth of the Neolithic Revolution support only artisans and traders: it also went to maintain priests and kings. By 3000 B.C. many highly organized cities were flourishing in the alluvial plains of the Tigris and Euphrates and the Nile valley. One can picture the winding streets between the mud-brick houses of the citizens – here a gem-cutter at work, there a potter spinning his wheel, weavers at their looms, a metallic tapping coming from the bronze-smith's anvil. There would be a market where country folk brought their produce – now increased by the invention of the man-driven plough to supersede the woman's hoe cultivation. And, dominating all, the great palace or temple or combination of the two, where the ruler and his satellites held power through a judicious blending of secular with magico-religious sanctions.

These vital changes in human existence were accomplished in the East while western Europe was still in the possession of the primitive Mesolithic food-gatherers described in the first chapter. But, however slowly, the results of the Neolithic Revolution could not fail to spread outward until they reached even the distant shores of Britain. Several urges combined to force this expansion of Neolithic culture. One was the increase in population which caused a perpetual demand for *lebensraum;* another was the quest for new sources of raw materials which drove ambitious prospectors and traders to explore and settle farther and farther afield. A third and most important urge was that of the peasants, who were for ever in quest of the fresh land which their primitive agriculture was forever exhausting.

By these means new centres of Neolithic settlement grew up in the Danube basin and along the Mediterranean, where in time they, too, became urbanized and developed their own elaborate civilizations. But the farther away from its source the Revolution spread the simpler its manifestations became, until in western Europe only mixed farming and the simplest crafts were introduced. The Iberian peninsula won some importance through its mineral wealth, and here alone in the west a few settlements were large enough almost to deserve the name of cities. It was from here, from Spain and Portugal, that we shall find parties of adventurers (p. 60) setting sail for the Atlantic coasts of Britain and Ireland. But these Iberian voyagers did not form the most substantial part of the Neolithic colonizers of this country. These rather were simple farming communities which, possibly originating in pre-dynastic Egypt, had spread from the south of France northwards and westwards until groups of them began to cross the Channel to reach our southern and eastern shores. They were slightly built, dark people, with long, rather narrow heads and delicate features, members of that ancient Mediterranean race that to-day can be seen at its purest among the southern Italians. We can visualize how parties of such men, women and children pushed off in their small boats from various points along the Channel and North Sea coast, taking with them cargoes of cattle, sheep and seed corn. Probably the Channel was still considerably narrower than to-day, and our cliffs would beckon a land-hungry people with promise of conditions similar to those they had enjoyed on the chalk of northern France. Once across the sea, the newcomers seem to have spread rapidly over the upland system (p. 17), reaching the Lincolnshire Wolds, Yorkshire, lowland Scotland and presently even across to northeast Ireland.

Now for the first time cultivated plots appeared on English hillsides, and domestic flocks and herds grazed the uplands. Now for the first time also men banded together to construct settlements, and then tombs, on such a scale that their handiwork is still visible, the earliest marks of human activity that survive on the face of this country.

Nearly a dozen of the distinctive entrenched settlements of the Neolithic period have been detected in southern England, from Devon to Sussex, the great majority of them on the chalk downs. The largest of them, and the most fully excavated, crowns Windmill Hill above the great temple at Avebury in Wiltshire, and, in recognition of its importance, the name of this site has been given to the culture as a whole: thus archaeologists speak, perhaps rather clumsily, of the Windmill Hill culture and Windmill Hill people. Another very interesting example lies under the racecourse on Whitehawk Hill above Brighton.

It is difficult to understand the purpose of the curious plan on which these oldest entrenchments were built. Several con-

centric rings of ditches and banks were dug with a considerable space between them, so that the area of the innermost
enclosure may be less than a quarter of the total space en-
circled by the outermost ring. The ditches themselves were
not continuous, but divided into short segments by solid
causeways of undisturbed soil, a peculiar feature which has
given these settlements the name of 'causewayed camps'. The
material dug from the ditches was piled along the inner lip to
form a bank that was sometimes crowned with a stockade.
Why the extraordinary number of entrances which the causewayed plan implies? Homer ascribes to the Egyptian Thebes
'a hundred gates from each of which sally forth two hundred
men', and it would be enlivening to transfer the scene to our
English camps. But it is most improbable that simple farmers
would use such military tactics; they are more likely to have
made the entrances for the convenience of cowherds who
wished to drive their cattle into the central area to keep them
safe from marauding men and beasts. Certainly no trace of
huts has ever been found in the central space, but instead the
usual occupation litter of broken crockery, vegetable refuse,
bones, dead dogs and the like lies in the ditches, suggesting
that the inhabitants lived in the shelter of the entrenchments,
penning the flocks and herds in their midst. Perhaps none of
these camps was ever permanently occupied; they may well
have been used only for one season of the year: the late
summer, when the cattle and sheep had to be herded for
branding and gelding.

In addition to the camps there must have been many isolated settlements dotted about the countryside, of which as
yet only a few are known. On Haldon in Devon a fair-sized
rectangular house with stone foundations has been uncovered, while on the hill of Carn Brea in Cornwall are the
remains of round stone huts, which are probably but not

certainly Neolithic. In the north of England quite a different type of dwelling existed at Ehenside Tarn in Cumberland, where Windmill Hill people lived in some kind of waterside settlement, paddling canoes, and perhaps catching eels with wooden tridents.

Near by the settlement we can imagine the women establishing their small gardens and corn-plots on the sunnier slopes, bending low as they tilled them with flint or stone hoes, with digging-sticks or antler picks. Their principal cereal crop was wheat, of which they grew two rather poor varieties, club wheat and emmer. When the women had gathered their modest harvest, they ground the grain in the simplest of mills, a small stone rubbed round and round by hand upon a much larger one, which in time acquired a convenient hollow top.

But of far greater importance to these people than their agriculture were the flocks and herds which the men tended and grazed on the hilltops and uncultivated slopes. Their cattle were fair-sized animals with wide-spreading horns, quite unlike the small shorthorn, *Bos longifrons*, which was to be introduced in the Bronze Age, but possibly the descendants of a cross between this breed and the great wild ox, *Bos primigenius*. The size of the herds was always limited by the wasteful necessity of slaughtering many head when grass failed in the autumn, a practice which lasted all through the Middle Ages, and could be abandoned only in the seventeenth century with the introduction of root-crops for winter feeding.

Pigs were commonly kept, and it may be supposed that they were encouraged to venture down into the forested valleys to root, and in season to fatten on acorns.

The herdsmen seem already to have used dogs to save their legs, a breed not unlike a long-legged fox terrier with small head and short back. They were evidently fed very largely on bones, for so rich were their droppings in calcium salts that they often hardened and survive for the diversion of visitors at present-day excavations.

Farm produce did not by any means entirely displace natural food supplies – men still went hunting, armed with bows and arrows tipped with fine, leaf-shaped flint heads, and brought back venison, birds and other small game to vary the round of beef, mutton and pork.

The domestic crafts practised by the Windmill Hill folk were simple and few – although it must never be forgotten that for every object that has survived the passage of 4000 years, scores made of perishable materials have disappeared without trace.

The women were exceptionally skilful potters, and their products make a worthy opening chapter to the long history of British ceramics. Working entirely by hand, they shaped round-bottomed bowls and jars, severely plain but usually well-proportioned and pleasing; the paste is often dark in colour, levigated with grits, and fine enough to allow quite thin walls and a well-smoothed, glossy surface (Fig. 4). They were always very sparing in their use of ornament, but occasionally would employ lines of pricks and incisions on shoulder or rim, or drag their finger-tips across the wet clay to produce a faintly fluted effect. Primitive potters are notoriously conservative, and little scope is left for individual taste – mothers would teach daughters their methods and designs, impressing upon them that theirs was the only right and proper way to make a pot, that any other would probably prove impossible and certainly unlucky. Nevertheless we do know of one Hampshire potter who, moved perhaps by a sudden whim or urge to assert herself, decorated a bowl by the imprint of a string of beads which we may imagine she took from her own neck.

49

In considering the reason for the rapid development of potting among Neolithic peoples, it is clear that with their flour pastes and milk their need for heat-proof and water-tight vessels was much more urgent than among the Palaeolithic and Mesolithic hunters who could cook most of their foods by simple roasting on spits.

Primitive pottery forms are often derived from vessels made in other materials – baskets, gourds and the like – and

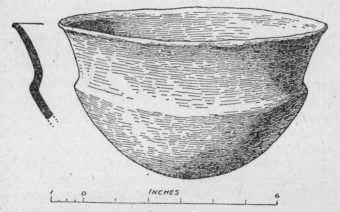

FIG. 4. Neolithic pottery bowl from the flint-mines at Cissbury, Sussex.

the simple baggy shapes favoured by the Windmill Hill potters may well have been copied from leather vessels; thus, though none of their products has survived, we can infer that these people were accomplished leather workers. Whether skins were also used for clothing is uncertain. There is no evidence for weaving earlier than the Bronze Age in this country, yet we know that it was practised by the continental kinsfolk of the Windmill Hill people, and it is most unlikely that they themselves had lost the art. Yet they would hardly have scorned the warmth of furs in winter time, and we may guess that some of their innumerable flint scrapers were used for cleaning and softening skins, which were then sewn with thongs threaded in bone needles.

Of Neolithic carpentry, again, very little survives, but the abundance of trees must have encouraged the use of wood. Shapely axe-hafts (Fig. 5, 1), clubs, paddles, a trident and the fragment of a wooden bowl from Ehenside Tarn give some slight idea of the mass of material that has perished elsewhere. No doubt also much more ambitious tasks were undertaken, such as the hollowing of boats and the dressing of timbers for house frames.

For many people the Neolithic period is rather drearily represented by the dusty rows of flints, sometimes of doubtful authenticity, which they have vaguely noticed in museum cases. Although this is an unfair conception due to the indestructibility of flint and the devoted persistence of amateur flint collectors, there is no doubt that the output of small implements must have been very great. Simple types, such as the scrapers that bulk so largely in all these collections, could presumably have been made by every man for himself, but the very fine craftsmanship shown in some of the leaf-shaped arrowheads suggests that they were the work of specially skilled individuals. When we come to that most important part of Neolithic accoutrement, the heavy flint or stone axes, adzes and picks, there is no longer any question that they were made by specialists who traded them among the peasant communities. They represent, in fact, the only essential import of these communities, the one gap in their economic self-sufficiency. This specialization was necessary not only because the shaping, grinding and polishing of such tools required much time and labour, but because their

FIG. 5. Neolithic stone axe in its wooden haft (Ehenside Tarn, Cumberland), and Early Bronze Age stone axe-hammer.

relatively large size and the need for strength demanded material that was not everywhere available.

The fine-grained stones that were particularly suitable had to be obtained from the highland zone; at Graig Lwyd in north Wales and the Langdale Pykes in Cumberland factories have been discovered where the local rock was used in such quantities that the hill-sides were strewn with the waste products of this ancient British industry. The Graig Lwyd axes were evidently of good quality, for they found purchasers as far afield as south Wales, Wessex and even Essex.

Still more remarkable was the organization required for the large-scale manufacture of flint axes, involving as it did elaborate mining operations. In order to reach the big nodules of readily workable flint that lay bedded in the chalk of southern and eastern England, pits were sunk to a depth of as much as fifty feet, often with underground galleries to follow up and exploit the richest seams (Fig. 6). The principal flint-mining centres were along the South Downs, particularly in the Worthing region, and in Norfolk at the famous site of Grime's Graves; other centres were established in Wessex. Once a good seam had been struck, shaft after shaft was sunk until several hundred might be found in a single group, often with their galleries linked together to form a vast, intricate network far below the ground. To-day such clusters show on the surface as a confused jumble of bumps and hollows not unlike a disused bombing field.

Excavation among them has given us some of the most intimate and vivid pictures of Neolithic life. We can imagine how the miners formed a caste set somewhat apart from their fellows, even as miners are to-day, by the mysterious and dangerous nature of their profession, toiling unseen where ordinary people dare not go. Laboriously they dug their pits, working with shovels made from the shoulder-blades of domestic animals, and with picks, hammers and wedges of antler, then, the flint-bed reached, drove their

Feet 10   5   0   10   20 Feet
R.G.

FIG. 6. Neolithic flint-mine (Harrow Hill, Sussex)
being cleared by modern excavators.

galleries crouching or lying prone as they prised out the valuable nodules. The miners must have grown familiar with the maze of their subterranean burrows, but when they were long and dark they lit them with little chalk lamps: simple cups probably containing fat and floating wick. In some of the Sussex mines black patches on the roof still mark the places where these lamps burnt with a smoky flame that must have filled the galleries with strange flickering shadows, and a powerful smell.

. The massive nodules, when at last they had been hoisted in baskets to the surface, were flaked into axes on the spot. Many workshops have been found, often in the shelter afforded by a partially filled shaft, where piles of flakes and wasters are proof of the mass production of a standardized tool-form.

A most dramatic find made recently at the bottom of one of the Grime's Graves pits leads on to the whole question of the magico-religious beliefs of Neolithic times. Enthroned on a ledge sat the chalk-carved image of a fat and pregnant woman, looking down on a phallus, also cut in chalk, and a great pile of deer-horn picks that had been laid as offerings at her feet. Here, in fact, was the shrine of a fertility cult, but one apparently intended to serve a curious and unexpected purpose. This particular shaft had failed to strike the usual rich flint-bed, and it seems reasonable to suppose that the shrine was set up to counteract the sterility of this pit and ensure the abundance of the next. But this was only one manifestation in the peculiar conditions of a mining community of a fertility cult that was generally practised among the Neolithic people – female figurines and phalli have been found at several causewayed camps and in a tomb, where presumably the rites were directed to more hopeful biological ends – the fecundity of men and beasts.

It is above all in tombs that we may hope to gain insight into religious belief and practice. In all Near Eastern and Mediterranean centres of civilization, and particularly in Egypt, labour and wealth were lavished on the dead to secure their contentment in the next world and hence goodwill towards their survivors in this. Equally in Britain, with their humbler resources, the Neolithic peasantry directed their greatest communal efforts to raising imposing tombs where generations of their dead could be worthily lodged.

The mausoleum most fashionable among the Windmill Hill people was the long barrow, an earthen mound or stone cairn built on a monumental scale that must have demanded great and well-organized labour. The stones piled into a long cairn would be at least enough to build the average parish church. Many long barrows are from 200 to 300 feet long and over 50 feet wide, and if nowadays they rarely stand more than 8 feet in height, this is in part due to the levelling processes of time.

The most familiar type of long barrow is the earthen one which has no visible architectural features. As we know them to-day (Pl. 2A), low, grassy, pear-shaped mounds lying among the lesser fry of Bronze Age round barrows, their construction looks simple enough, but when they were in commission many had structures, since collapsed, which must have given them a certain architectural quality. Such structures might include a curving façade of stout timbers across the wider end and side walls of turf or posts rising above deep flanking ditches. In some of them, too, the larger end covered some form of wooden chamber in which many bodies might be buried together.

The great majority of these earthen long barrows are to be seen along the southern chalk from Sussex to Dorset, but there are other interesting groups on the Yorkshire and Lincolnshire Wolds. A freakish example discovered below the Iron Age camp at Maiden Castle in Dorset deserves special mention, for it not only reached the fantastic length of nearly one-third of a mile, but contained a dismembered corpse that had evidently been jointed and had its skull split open to play the central rôle at a ritual feast – probably with the intention that the feasters should absorb with his flesh something of the dead man's qualities and might. But such customs cannot have been very usual among our forebears; burial in the barrows was commonly by simple inhumation, the body being crouched, perhaps to represent the natural position of sleep, or possibly to recall the foetal attitude in preparation for a rebirth after death. Sometimes, however, cremation was practised, most conspicuously in Yorkshire, where the long barrows were at times raised over specially designed trenches in which the corpses had been burnt on pyres of wood.

Another region famous for its long barrows is the Cotswold country, especially to the west, where along the steep scarp fronting the Severn a number are set on jutting headlands, where they can command superbly the great spreading expanse of the valley. These Cotswold barrows are not mere earthen mounds, like the majority in Sussex and Wessex; the local oolitic rock was available for the building of long cairns of neatly piled slabs, held in place with drystone walling and covering elaborate burial chambers formed with huge stone blocks or 'megaliths'. There was an essential difference in the use of this chambered type of tomb. The earthen form was a communal grave, in that it contained a number of bodies all interred simultaneously, but the stone chamber was a collective tomb intended for successive burials over a long period of time. Possibly the privilege of burial in these imposing monuments was limited to ruling families (all the skeletons in the chamber of one Wiltshire barrow showed a strong family likeness), a state of affairs that exists to-day, when the possession of a family vault is certainly an upper-class prerogative.

One of the best preserved and finest of these chambered long barrows is the charmingly named Hetty Pegler's Tump, near Uley, and a visit there is not soon forgotten. To enter one must stoop to pass below a massive lintel, supported on two upright blocks, into a gallery from which side cells open on either hand between towering pillars. And these few steps carry one from the familiar, brightly lit Cotswold scene into a strange cave world, with dark, shadowy entrances and a lingering ghostly presence in the air that may be felt only by the imagination but is none the less potent for that. Indeed, he would be a stone who in such an atmosphere is not tempted to materialize before him the men who once moved about in this cave of their own making, who cannot see a party of them coming through the low portal, staggering a little from the weight of the corpse which they are bearing to its sepulchre. Lifting it into one of the side-chambers, they must move aside the bones of earlier ancestors before they can deposit the body of their tribesman lying on its side with knees drawn up to chin. After celebrating the last rites and leaving with the body a few ornaments, and perhaps a bow and arrow and some pots holding food and drink, they withdraw, and carefully seal up the entrance behind them. So it will lie hidden until the day of the next funeral, but the site of the entrance remains a centre for ritual, where offerings may be laid and the ancestral spirits be propitiated or invoked.

Its ritual significance heightened the architectural importance of the portal, and when in some of the later Cotswold barrows the great central chamber was abandoned in favour of smaller cells let into the sides of the mound, the forecourt and portal were still set up, dummies leading nowhere, but providing a stage for the performance of the traditional rites.

The Cotswold barrows form only a part of a larger group of chambered long barrows centring round the Bristol Channel and the Severn. There are a number in south Wales, the best known being that called after St Nicholas, not very far from Cardiff. There are also a few eastern outliers, including the most famous of the whole group, Wayland's Smithy, that lies so beautifully on the Berkshire Downs about a mile's walk along the great Ridgeway from the equally famous White Horse of Uffington. The popularity of this grave is due more to the romantic name of Wayland than to its own inherent interest; strange that a figure so essentially of the Iron age as this legendary blacksmith, who would shoe your horse for a groat left on the roof of the smithy, should become attached to a tomb raised by a people not yet familiar even with bronze.

The Cotswold and related long barrows are not by any means the only megalithic tombs in Britain: there are hundreds, built in a variety of shapes and sizes, to be seen in the highland zone from Land's End to the Orkneys. The conspicuous manner in which they cluster along the coasts and round inland waterways with easy access from the sea suggests at once that they owed their inspiration to a maritime people who made the Atlantic and the Irish Sea their highway. Such a sea going tradition was something so alien to the Windmill Hill peasant population that we must evidently look elsewhere for the originators of this Cyclopean architecture, and the direction to which we should turn is southwards, towards the more advanced civilizations of the Mediterranean.

The idea of building collective tombs with great stone slabs seems first to have been adopted in the western Mediterranean, where they were probably copied from similarly planned vaults hewn out of the solid rock. The mental conception underlying the idea is obscure: some have suggested that the tombs were intended as substitutes for natural caves, others that they were houses for the dead adapted from the houses of the living, others again have even ventured to recognize them as a rendering of the womb from which the spirits of the dead were to be reborn.

Whatever the explanation, it is certain that after about 2300 B.C. men were occupied in raising such monuments for their dead in Sicily, Sardinia, southern France, Spain and Portugal. From these centres the practice was carried to the distant lands of the west and north – to Brittany and our own coasts, and then onwards to the shores of the Baltic – until by 2000 B.C. it must have been possible to sail the hundreds of miles from southern Spain to Sweden finding along the whole route the coasts in possession of people sharing this cultural tradition in common. But there the uniformity stopped: it is unlikely that the bulk of the megalith-building folk in the different regions would have been found to speak the same language, and they certainly did not have any common tradition for the manufacture of their tools, weapons and pottery. For it seems that the dissemination of megaliths can be likened to that of a religion, accomplished by a comparatively small number of 'missionaries' who made converts of, and came to dominate, the local populations of many lands. We can see these elaborate tombs as everywhere merely the solid and enduring setting for a ritual cult with its own powerful magic. Visual proof of such a widespread cult is given by the curious symbolic patterns of magical significance that are carved on many megaliths in Iberia, Brittany, Ireland and Wales, and sometimes reproduced on sepulchral pottery. Doubtless such missionaries were by no means so exclusively preoccupied with holy things as the later Celtic saints, who followed much the same routes to spread the Christian gospel and Christian architecture – their travels may have been very largely prompted by economic motives.

Nevertheless they owed their success and their easy domination of native peoples to the supposed magical power that went with their control of the megalithic cult. In Britain they seem, for instance, to have had no difficulty in establishing a control of some of the Windmill Hill peasants, whose labour must have been employed for the moving and raising of the great blocks and collecting the tons of stone that went into the covering cairns.

Just as Christian churches were built to many plans at different times and among different sects – from the Orthodox basilica and the Catholic cruciform cathedral to the pseudo-romanesque Ebenezer and the tin chapel – so different groups of megalith builders believed in the virtue of their own distinctive types of tomb. Two principal plans were followed in western and northern Europe, the 'passage grave', in which a circular or rectangular chamber roofed with slabs or corbelling is approached through a narrow passage, and the 'long cist' or 'covered gallery grave', which consists simply of a long, parallel-sided burial chamber with no distinct passageway.

Both these plans are found in the British Isles, together with a host of variations from them, either in the direction of greater elaboration, or, more commonly, of degeneration due to lack of materials and labour or a decline in the zeal of the faithful.

The most ambitious and successful architects were among the followers of the passage-grave tradition whose labour and skill have given us some of the most magnificent monuments of our prehistory (Pl. 1A). Many of their greatest achievements are in Ireland, where passage-grave territory stretched to the north-west across central Ireland from the east coast, and of them all the most justly famous is the tomb of New Grange in Co. Meath. Here a huge circular cairn

280 feet in diameter and ringed with a circle of standing stones, conceals a beautifully masoned megalithic grave no less than 80 feet long, its walls and threshold (Pl. 1B) enriched with an intricate medley of magical carvings. But this is merely an outstanding example among a number of remarkable Irish graves, which are sometimes to be seen grouped together in cemeteries.

The school of megalithic art so well exemplified by the New Grange carvings can be recognized as the first important non-representational art of western Europe, and one which arose in the service of religion. Although all its motifs were derived by gradual stylization from representations of men and animals, they became at last almost entirely geometric. When reproduced incoherently as scattered patterns without any unity of composition, their purely symbolic purpose was evidently uppermost in the mind of the designer, but when, as at New Grange, there was some attempt at a general composition, the sculptor must have been genuinely concerned with the visual effect of his work as decoration. It is an art which cannot claim any great merit, which cannot for a moment stand comparison with the naturalistic masterpieces of the palaeolithic hunters; nevertheless at its best it achieved a certain effectiveness, and merits some attention as the sole expression to have survived of any serious decorative purpose before the growth of the beautiful secular art of the Celts nearly 2000 years later.

The men who introduced passage-grave architecture and art seem to have reached Ireland from Portugal and southwest Spain and to have brought with them an interest in trade and metallurgy, including gold prospecting, which distinguished them from their more pedestrian contemporaries preoccupied with the production of food. From Ireland some sailed for Scotland and, settling along the natural trade route offered by the line of the Great Glen, in time established a traffic in early copper implements – axes and halberds – then for the first time becoming sought after in Britain. Others, again, *en route* for Scandinavia, colonized the Western Isles and more intensively the extreme north of Scotland and the Orkneys.

Maeshowe in those islands is comparable in grandeur with New Grange, and is so similar in construction that it must surely have been raised for a chiefly family hailing from Ireland, or even from Spain itself. Had the grave goods survived, they could have given more certain information on this point, but it so happened that some 300 years after the building of the tomb it was robbed by a band of Vikings who chanced to shelter there. Perhaps benighted or caught by a storm on the moorlands, they must have made their way to the great round artificial hill that dominated the flat landscape, and with mingled superstitious dread and bravado have groped along the 40 feet of passage-way to reach the spacious cruciform chamber, where perhaps no one had set foot since the last funerary procession withdrew some three millennia before. One can feel gratitude to these Norsemen for whiling away the time by cutting a runic record of their visit on the stones, even while reviling them for the habit of plunder which prompted them to empty the grave of all trace of its original possessors.

The adherents to the rival megalithic sect of the covered gallery appear to have approached Britain from the south of France and the Pyrenees, whence their connexions can be traced even farther east in the peculiar 'Giants' Graves' of Sardinia. Sailing up the Irish Sea or round the west coast, they settled on either side of the narrows of the North Channel – in south-west Scotland, Ulster, and Man, where geographical conditions (p. 18) often dictated their splitting up into small communities, each farming a fertile valley or strip of coast. They did not strive after such ambitious architectural effects as the passage-grave people, and their tombs differ from passage graves in that they seem hardly to have been designed as buildings in which men could move freely about. Not only was the roof inclined to be low, but in many Scottish examples the cist was divided into small compartments by transverse slabs, over which it would only be possible to wriggle in a difficult and undignified manner.

As with the Cotswold chambered barrows, the covering mound was usually long in shape, and the centre of interest tended to be focused on a portal, which in the most elaborate examples was formed by two large uprights set at the centre of a semicircular façade recessed in one end of the cairn. This forecourt, a more ornate version of the splayed entrance of the Cotswold chambered barrows, must have been planned for use, and it is not too fanciful to see it filled by a circle of dancers moving in some revolving figure, while offerings might be made at the portal to propitiate the spirits of the ancestors who dwelt within.

A tomb of this type on St Kilda has been reported; it is a profoundly romantic thought that 4000 years ago men and women may have reached and maintained themselves upon this island 50 miles out into the Atlantic, beyond even the outer Hebrides – an island recently abandoned as too remote for human habitation. These were adventurers indeed, fearless of the sea, of the unknown, of utter isolation.

The long-cist people did not follow the passage-grave practice of decorating their tombs with sacred patterns, but instead sometimes engraved the same designs on their sepulchral pottery. This joint possession of a common symbolism shows the underlying unity of the megalithic belief, much as the symbols of the cross and chi-ro monogram could be used to demonstrate the common Christian doctrines shared by the Catholic and Orthodox Churches. Indeed, that they were not irreconcilably torn by sectarian bigotry is shown in areas such as the Hebrides, where the passage-grave and long-cist people met and so far united as to produce a hybrid architectural tradition which presumably reflects a parallel doctrinal compromise.

There remains a small megalithic group, of which Kit's Coty House is, by reason of another attractive name, the most familiar, isolated far from the main western centres of the highland zone in the Medway valley of Kent. They had small, box-like chambers in long mounds enclosed by rectangular palings of upright stones, and are interesting because they were never directly connected with the main stream of the megalithic movement round the Atlantic and Irish Sea coasts, but were inspired by immigrants from across the North Sea, from the Low Countries and north-west Germany, where the so-called 'Huns' Beds' are very similar in design.

The Windmill Hill peasants, with their causewayed camps and long barrows, and the megalith-building chiefs who dominated them in the west, were the sections of Neolithic society that have left us monumental reminders of their existence. But there was a third people, destined to emerge and grow in importance during the coming millennium, whose less advanced economic and social organization prevented them from leaving any such striking monuments to call them to mind. These are the Peterborough people, largely descendants of the old Mesolithic inhabitants of Britain, who, while adopting certain Neolithic accomplishments such as potting, herding and simple husbandry, continued to follow the old mode of life as hunters and fishers. With the fair northern colouring which this ancestry would have given them, they must have differed strikingly from their more swarthy Mediterranean contemporaries. And at first they were able to hold themselves apart, for they were dominant in the east, while the Windmill Hill folk were mainly concentrated in the south and west, and while the Windmill Hill people were attracted to the uplands, they preferred life in river valleys, by marshes and the sea-coast. However, the two stocks naturally did encounter one another, particularly when after a time the Peterborough range extended farther westward. Their cultures are occasionally found mingled in Sussex and Wessex. They probably met, too, over trading ventures, for not only did the Peterborough people take some share in flint-mining, but it appears that they were the distributors, and probably also the manufacturers, of the Graig Lwyd axes from north Wales (p. 53). The adoption of distributive trading as a side-line by a hunting people is not altogether unexpected, as their few domestic ties would allow them the necessary mobility.

Very little is known of Peterborough settlements, doubtless because their houses tended to be impermanent and flimsy, and they had no conception of communal planning on the scale of a causewayed camp. The only known dwellings are round huts very much like those that sheltered their Mesolithic predecessors, with floors sunk a little into the ground and walled and roofed with small interwoven branches.

As potters the women were not highly skilled. They employed the 'coiled' method, by which long sausages of clay are laid in coils, then squeezed together and moulded with the fingers. In contrast with the Windmill Hill pottery, which at its best is so well made and unornate, the Peterborough woman favoured lavish ornament on coarse, clumsy and often ill-fired vessels, generally round-bottomed bowls, with a thick rim and deeply hollowed neck. The ornament was produced by impressing the soft clay with twisted or whipped cord, the finger-nail, the serrated edge of a shell or the end of a small bird bone, and was scattered with more zest than discrimination over the entire surface of the pot. When, as we have seen, the Peterborough people encountered their neighbours, one of the tangible results was the adoption by the Windmill Hill potters of the idea of fairly free decoration, although they always used it with some restraint and applied it to their own superior wares.

Among Peterborough flint specialities the most interesting are arrow-heads with a broad cutting edge instead of a point, and the sickle, generally a parallel-sided blade slightly curved at the tip, specimens of which have been found with a lustre along the cutting edge that can have been produced only by friction against cornstalks.

It may be supposed that a relationship of mutual toleration mingled with mutual scorn existed between the Peterborough and Windmill Hill tribes in so far as they had any concern with one another. The uplanders would despise the valley-dwellers as poor irreligious natives with no idea of organized existence, its duties and advantages, while the valley folk might well feel that their contemporaries had sacrificed much of their freedom to a monotonous and restricted way of life, and much of the wealth thus won to an unprofitable and unnecessary preoccupation with their dead.

It would be hard to over-stress the importance of the span of British history covered by this chapter. A rural economy already containing the germs of ours of to-day was suddenly imposed from without on a primitive society that had changed very little for some 20,000 years. This Neolithic settlement was, in fact, the first of the long series of contacts between Britain and the higher civilizations of the Mediterranean which have played so stimulating a part in the development of our culture. It ranks in importance beside such later influences as those of the Roman Empire, the Christian Church and the Renaissance.

The ensuing Bronze and Iron Ages were to bring great advances in material achievement, but nothing so fundamental as this revolution from a food-hunting to a food-producing basis for society. The growth of metallurgy and the immense improvement in equipment which it permitted, and the commercial development which it demanded, were certainly important, but it was only from soil prepared by the Neolithic economy that this growth could ever have sprung.

CHAPTER III

The Early and Middle Bronze Ages

THE terms Stone Age, Bronze Age and Iron Age devised more than a hundred years ago have proved of lasting value, and their very simplicity has an appeal for the ear and the imagination. Yet they should be accepted only with discretion. It must not be supposed that everywhere and all at once men abandoned their stone tools and scorned to use anything but bronze, or forgot bronze as soon as the smelting of iron had been perfected. Even to-day, with our vastly accelerated rate of material progress, we can see overlaps between and old world and a new; electricity has still failed to displace the candle from many cottages, the tractor has by no means driven the horse-drawn plough off the fields, and by going only as far afield as the Hebrides one can see corn still being ground in a stone hand-quern. In all such instances primitive forms have survived the Industrial Revolution through a combination of distance from the urban centres of civilization with poverty, often strongly reinforced by individual conservatism. These factors have always operated, and it is not surprising that in days before organized production and distribution, and before advertising, the adoption of any innovation was slow indeed. Stone tools kept a place in man's equipment through the longer part of the Bronze Age, and the majority of the stray flint implements that are hopefully assigned to the Neolithic in a host of private and some public collections were really shaped after the introduction of metal.

We have already seen how copper was in free use in the East before even Neolithic culture reached Britain, and how the first interest in metallurgy in these islands seems to have been among the passage-grave people who had settled in the Highland Zone. With copper at hand in Ireland and in lesser quantities in Scotland, and one of the most important European sources of tin easily accessible in Cornwall, the smiths of the Highland Zone were favourably placed, and they were certainly at work casting copper and bronze implements well before metallurgy was practised in lowland England.

The adoption of metal tools in England was to be accelerated by an event of outstanding importance in our prehistory: the invasion of a fresh warrior race from the Continent. These people were not themselves great metallurgists, but they provided a ready and expanding new market for the Irish smiths, and for this reason their arrival from about 1900 B.C. is recognized as opening the British Early Bronze Age.

Archaeological whim has attached a variety of labels to the prehistoric peoples whose own names have been lost for ever: it may choose a representative site such as Windmill Hill, but sometimes a particularly characteristic item in the people's equipment is selected. Thus these first Bronze Age invaders are known as Beaker Folk, from a highly distinctive type of pot in common use among them (Pl. 3A).

Like Neanderthal Man, the Beaker Folk have been the subject of many word-portraits, in which their virility is painted with powerful adjectives. Their strong bones, muscularity, pronounced brows and determined chins have all been emphasized, perhaps over-emphasized, while special stress has very properly been laid on the round form of their skulls, which contrasts so strongly with the neat, long heads of their Neolithic predecessors.

The previous migrations of the Beaker Folk on the Continent are among the most remarkable to have been traced by archaeology. It seems that the early cradle of the race was in inland Spain, where they were building their culture while the more advanced Megalithic people (p. 60) occupied the surrounding coasts. When pressure from their neighbours provoked an expansion from their homeland, one wing followed the Atlantic coast route to Brittany and the Channel Islands, and it would seem to have been from here that the first wave of Beaker Folk sailed for Britain. Making their main landings round the mouth of the Avon and the Stour, they quickly overran the good lands of the Wessex chalk. But meanwhile yet larger numbers of Beaker people had been spreading east and north from Spain, colonizing the islands and shores of the western Mediterranean and thrusting through both east France and north Italy to the heart of Europe. Here in central Europe and the middle Rhine they encountered and mingled with an even more warlike stock, the Battle-Axe people, who had wielded this weapon to establish their race and their speech over wide territories from the Black Sea to the Baltic. In race these Battle-Axe warriors can be called 'Nordic', while their languages belonged to that great Aryan or Indo-European family from which all the main modern European tongues descend. It was men and women in whose veins these two streams of adventurous blood were united who sailed from the Low Countries across the Channel and the North Sea to reach our coasts all the way from Sussex and Kent to northern Scotland. They came in several groups, of which the last to arrive was the most numerous and powerful, and also that in which the Battle-Axe element was strongest.

Once arrived, these several waves of energetic conquerors soon occupied the greater part of Britain, ruthlessly dispossessing the Neolithic communities of their best pastures, and also no doubt of their herds, and sometimes of their women. Though largely ousted from the English lowlands, the

Windmill Hill people survive as a physical strain in our population – that small, dark type common in the west and often mistakenly called 'Celtic' – but their culture was so thoroughly submerged that they disappeared from history, leaving only the slightest contributions to Bronze Age civilization.

The Peterborough people fared better, for with their different economy (p. 65) they had no need to compete directly with the newcomers for living space, and so survived to emerge triumphant after the force of the Beaker conquest was spent – much as the Anglo-Saxons reasserted themselves after the Norman Conquest.

But that force, while it lasted, was very great, and carried a few Beaker colonists even as far as Ireland in the west and the Orkneys in the north, although their numbers were too small to leave any very strong mark on these farthest outposts. It is an astonishing migration this, astonishing that a race fostered in a Mediterranean country should be able to trek to central Europe and become familiar with the Continental conditions of the Danube and the Rhine before pushing on to the most distant Atlantic shores and to islands already looking towards the Arctic. And during all this time and over all this distance they maintained their own material culture so little changed that if four sherds of beaker pottery from Spain and Bohemia, from Holland and Scotland were ranged on the palm of one's hand it might be impossible to distinguish between them.

It is not surprising to find that this restless folk, perhaps largely nomadic, were herdsmen basically dependent on their cattle, although always with a lively interest in trade. Agriculture had a place of minor importance in their economy. For dwellings tents were probably commonly used, but occasionally at least shallow circular or sub-rectangular pits were sunk into the ground and roofed perhaps with wattle, while it is likely that some of the familiar hut-circles that thrust through the Scottish and other moorland heather mark the stone foundations of Beaker dwellings.

With tools and weapons they were certainly better equipped than their predecessors, particularly in their possession of metal implements, few and simple though these were. Some of their equipment the first invaders may have brought with them from the Continent, but soon the Beaker Folk became the customers of the smiths of the Highland Zone, and particularly of the Irish smiths, from whom they purchased flat copper axes, awls, and both tanged and riveted daggers made to their own design.

This metal equipment was reinforced by implements of flint and stone. Finely chipped, tanged flint daggers were frequent substitutes for the copper and bronze forms which they imitated, and a roughly circular flint knife with the cutting edge well ground and polished was also popular. The ordinary polished axe remained in full use, while in addition the strong eastern group of Beaker Folk showed their Battle-Axe inheritance by carrying a stone axe-hammer pierced with a shaft-hole (Fig. 5, bottom), which is a simplified version of the more martial-looking continental forms.

All the Beaker people were archers, tipping their arrows with barbed flint heads and sometimes protecting their wrists from the sharp blow of the returning bow-string with stone guards: a Yorkshire warrior of wealth could afford the added elegance of gold nails to fix such a guard to its leather wristlet.

For fastening their dress they followed the prevalent Mediterranean fashion for buttons, a low, conical form being usual, sometimes carved from glossy black Yorkshire jet and embellished with a cruciform design. Jet was also used for the simple rings that acted as belt-fasteners. How much one would like to know what type of clothing such belts and buttons secured!

It seems that both linen and woollen fabrics were worn, at least by a fortunate few, for their remains have been found in graves, and it can hardly be supposed that the dead would enjoy a monopoly of these luxuries. Some few of the well-to-do also were able to deck themselves with ornaments of Irish gold, and so for the first time in Britain display that shining yellow badge that in one form or another was to remain the coveted insignia of wealth and power.

In the manufacture of the distinctive pots after which this people has been named the women showed very considerable skill, if little artistic sensibility. The paste is fine and hard, and in firing has often been allowed to oxidize to a pleasant reddish colour. Despite the really remarkable uniformity of beaker ware over its whole range, slight local variations could hardly fail to arise, and three main types were made by the different British groups. The high, expanding neck of one variety (Pl. 3A) is due to influence from the ceramic traditions of the Battle-Axe people. The ornament, usually ranged in horizontal bands and limited to a few geometric patterns of rather niggling effect, was often in finely dotted lines produced by the imprint of a toothed implement, although cord impressions and simple incisions were also employed.

Were these vessels really beakers in the sense of being primarily designed for drinking? It is very probable that they were, and it has even been suggested that they were intended for some fermented drink which helped the invaders to establish their mastery, rather as whisky has often opened the way for the less scrupulous white settlers in Africa and the Pacific, although the spiritual or magical power of alcohol may have been of greater importance.

74

If the Beaker Folk have left practically no domestic monuments, we are greatly indebted to them for those which they raised in the name of religion. Although never lavishing the same excessive labour on their tombs as the Neolithic communities, funerary ritual was by no means neglected. The old idea of communal burial, however, had little appeal to these roving warriors, and their dead were buried singly, crouching with the knees so close to the chin that the corpses must have been trussed into position (as in Pl. 2B). With them they laid an equipment for the next world suitable to the wealth they had owned in this: perhaps a dagger, bows and arrows, and any ornaments that the men and women had worn during life, and in addition almost invariably they added a beaker which we can hope was left brimming with a drink potent to cheer the unknown road of death. (It is good to recollect that less than fifty years ago a Lincolnshire widow insisted on burying with him her husband's favourite beer mug.)

Very occasionally such burials might be grouped in flat cemeteries, but the traditional rite was the piling over the grave of a round mound or cairn in the shape of an inverted bowl. A number of the round barrows that are so often seen strung across the sky-lines of the chalk downs (Pl. 6), and the round cairns that dot the moorlands, were raised over our Beaker ancestors. Sometimes the mounds cover a ring of posts that appear to represent a ritual house, occasionally they have been raised over an actual dwelling – presumably the dead man's own hut.

These barrows alone make a great contribution to the inheritance of our countryside, to the sights which in a passing moment may suddenly call the past to vivid life and fill us with a sense of ageless continuity. But still more should we thank the Beaker people for the foundation of two of our finest monuments: temples which as landmarks in our architectural history stand out in their period as Westminster Abbey or St Paul's in ours. Indeed, Avebury and Stonehenge are two of the most remarkable survivals from prehistoric times to be seen in western Europe. Avebury, near Marlborough, though less well known, is surely the more impressive of the two: it is almost incredible that a small population furnished with humble tools of wood, bone and stone should have the audacity to plan on such a magnificent scale. In its final form this temple comprised two pairs of concentric circles of huge stones weighing many tons apiece, standing side by side within a single stone circle, the largest of its kind in Europe, which was itself enclosed by a vast ring ditch embanked on its outer lip (Pl. 4A). The labour absorbed by this earthwork must have been immense. The chalk-cut ditch has a wide, flat bottom no less than 50 feet below the crest of the bank, and encloses an area of $28\frac{1}{2}$ acres. Nor is this the whole design. Southward an avenue of pairs of stones, whose alternating tall slender and short squat shapes are thought to be male and female symbols, follows a slightly zigzag course down to the river Kennet, and thence to Overton Hill, where it terminates in another sacred enclosure known as the Sanctuary. Against the bases of two of the great stones in this avenue, and within the Sanctuary, the bodies of Beaker Folk had been buried in the usual crouched position.

The great antiquary Stukeley, who visited Avebury in the early eighteenth century, when it was much more nearly complete, records that a second avenue left the main circle to the south-west, but of this, if it ever existed, there is now little sign. Stukeley, whose early aptitude for realistic observation was overcome in later life by the growing romanticism of his century, contrived to see in the plan of Avebury the symbol of a snake, of which this south-western avenue was the tail and the Overton Sanctuary the head. Without following him into these extremes of romantic interpretation, we may legitimately allow the imagination some freedom in picturing the ceremonies for which this colossal temple was designed. We can suppose that on days of festival the uninitiated worshippers congregated on the bank to watch across the great gulf of the ditch the priests performing their mysteries on the sacred ground of the inner circles, much as a Roman audience watched gladiatorial shows from the tiered seats of an amphitheatre. What these mysteries were we shall never know; the sun certainly played some part, but did it serve only to fix the time of the festivals, or was it the actual object of their worship? There is other evidence for sun-cults in the Bronze Age, while the earth goddess and phallic fertility rites which preoccupied the mind of Neolithic man seem to have lost their hold. There was a shift of interest from the earth and the womb upwards to the sun and the heavens – well symbolized by the change from the dark, closed tomb to the open, sun-orientated temple as the principal architectural form. This change is exactly what known religious history would lead one to expect. It is typical of Indo-European religion that Zeus, a sky god, should rule the Greek pantheon. So it was the strong Indo-European element infused into our Beaker culture by the Battle-Axe warriors (p. 71) which gave its religion this skyward trend. We are witnessing the triumph of some more barbaric Zeus over the ancient Earth Mother dear to the Neolithic peasantry, the goddess whom they had brought with them from the centres of her fertile power in the Mediterranean and the Near East.

Everyone who has been to Avebury has also seen Silbury Hill. There it stands, less than a mile from the temple, in a slight circular hollow, like a steamed pudding dished up for a giant. One hundred and thirty feet high, with a base covering more than five acres, it is the largest artificial mound in western Europe. From its appearance it might well be a huge barrow built over some outstanding Early Bronze Age celebrity, but a shaft sunk from top to bottom in the eighteenth century and a tunnel driven from ground-level in the nineteenth, followed by some recent trenching, have discovered virtually nothing. Its purpose and its age remain a riddle.

Stonehenge (Pl. 4B) has always been the most visited of our prehistoric monuments; remember, for instance, the trouble and expense which Pepys endured to inspect it when on his holiday jaunt to the west country, while a host of antiquaries and artists from Tudor times onwards have left us descriptions and delightful if inaccurate engravings. Yet it can never have been so magnificent as the complete Avebury, for despite the astonishing size of its stones the whole conception was far less bold – the entire sacred area being less than one-thirteenth as great. The easiest way to recall the complexities of Stonehenge is to approach it from without. It would be following in many prehistoric footsteps to mount up to it from the river Avon along the mile-and-a-half course of the 'avenue' enclosed between its two parallel banks and ditches, for this was a road which must often have been trodden when the temple was a living centre of religion. Led by the avenue to the north-east side of the monument, one crosses the low bank and ditch by its single entrance and, walking over the ring of empty socket-holes that has been uncovered just inside the bank, passes through the great outer circle of sarsen stones and that of 'bluestones' within, to find oneself entering between the arms of a double horseshoe, the outer one formed of five colossal trilithons, the inner of small 'bluestones'. And there, across the toe of this innermost bluestone horseshoe, lies the seeming centrepiece of the whole temple, the recumbent slab of the 'altar stone' on which popular imagination has offered up many bloody victims. Standing by this altar and looking back along the axis of the horseshoes to the 'Hele Stone' at the head of the avenue, one is facing the point where the sun will rise on midsummer day.

A pitch of architectural refinement was achieved at Stonehenge unparalleled in the prehistoric west. The transverse slabs which make a continuous architrave round the outermost sarsen ring are not only curved lengthwise to fit the circumference of the circle, but grow broader towards the top to compensate for the foreshortening when viewed from the ground. In addition, they, like the cross slabs of the trilithons, are secured by mortices hollowed out to fit over tenons projecting from the tops of the uprights. All this detail becomes the more remarkable when it is remembered that enormous patience must have been required to shape such stones with no better tool than a clumsy stone maul.

The bluestones, though dwarfed by the towering sarsens about them, are in fact no less remarkable. Geology has shown that they were brought here from Pembrokeshire, whence they were probably carried most of the way by sea. This journey of at least 200 miles gives insight alike into the unexpected possibilities of prehistoric transport and the great sanctity which must already in Wales have hallowed the bluestones to prompt such a prodigious undertaking.

It is a source of mortification to archaeologists that the two monuments about which they are most often questioned, Stonehenge and Silbury Hill, are precisely those which have been most tenacious of their secrets. In the case of Stonehenge this is partly due to the pre-scientific digging which its fame attracted. For intance, one recent excavator, on lifting a fallen slab in search of dating evidence, found instead a bottle of port wine generously laid down by an earlier investigator. However, despite such set-backs, certain facts are well established. The bank and ditch, together with the circle of empty sockets immediately within, are the earliest surviving features, and were the handiwork of the Beaker Folk. The sarsen horseshoe and ring were the next to be set up, apparently by the Wessex aristocracy, whose arrival from Brittany about 1500 B.C. will be related below (p. 91), and last of all the bluestones were put, evidently as part of the same scheme, in their present positions inside the sarsen ring. They had previously stood either on or near the site, possibly on the line of the neighbouring earthwork known as The Cursus. How long a period is covered by these additions and alterations to the fabric of the temple is hard to estimate precisely, but it is most likely that they were completed during the earlier part of the Bronze Age. What, then, of the Druids, those mysterious priests of the Celtic Iron Age with whose bearded and long-robed figures many of us have loved to people the great circles of Stonehenge? The fountain-head for such picturesque ideas was in the imagination of Stukeley (Druids had an inevitable appeal to a Romantic), and for this reason it was long the pleasurable duty of the scientific mind to scorn and deny them. Yet the discovery of undoubted Iron Age pottery on the site, and also (as will be seen later, p. 161) of Iron Age stone holes, has shaken such scepticism. It is now possible and permissible to believe that there must have been a last phase when Stonehenge was administered by Celtic priests, although they had little share in its devising. It seems, then, that Stukeley's hazards were really nearer the truth than he deserved.

These two great centres of worship, demanding such heavy labour and such feats of transport and engineering to build, must not be dismissed without thought of their social implications. It is clear that the acceptance of such tasks implies an immense compelling power in religion, and possibly one fostered and directed by a strong priesthood. But more than that, the ability to command such labour and the fact that the temples evidently served a considerable population and wide territories must mean some degree of social and political organization. This is the counterpart of the cultural uniformity imposed upon Britain by the Beaker conquest, and is implicit also in the far-flung commercial contacts of the conquering overlords: their ability to obtain gold, copper and bronze from Ireland, Yorkshire jet, greenstone from Brittany. Here is the liquidation for all time of the small, self-sufficient social units of the old Neolithic era.

Stonehenge and Avebury were not, of course, the only sacred buildings of their kind, but the outstanding examples of a large class varying widely both in age and construction. It is possible that a simple kind of embanked sanctuary was already being made in late Neolithic times, and it has been suggested that the variety with a single entrance through bank and ditch is older than those with two or more. Opinion about these monuments is, in fact, still very uncertain, but at least there is no doubt that it was the Beaker peoples who developed them into striking and original architectural form. The tradition of the enclosing earthwork and perhaps also of wooden posts is at home in a stoneless lowland country and may be attributed to the Battle-Axe element among the Beaker groups who came to Britain from the east (p. 71); the stone circle on the other hand was proper to the highlands of the Atlantic seaboards where there was not only the necessary material but also a long-established practice of megalithic architecture. The two traditions met and mingled in Britain to produce the combinations of stone settings and earthworks which are among the noblest of our prehistoric monuments.

A remarkable example of a sanctuary with embankment and wooden settings is Woodhenge, lying not far from Stonehenge, where the bank and ditch enclosed no fewer than six concentric ovals of posts, their long axis orientated on the midsummer sunrise. Here grim evidence was forthcoming of the savage demands made by primitive religion: buried on the axis of the innermost sanctuary was the skeleton of a baby whose head had been cleft open when it was offered as a sacrifice, probably at the dedication of the temple.

Another site where the eastern type of architecture is naturally found in its purest form is at Arminghall near Norwich. This monument must in its day have been most impressive, for within its double ditch was a horseshoe setting of gigantic oak trunks, sunk 7 feet into the ground and probably rising as much as 20 feet above it. Kindred embanked monuments can be seen at Gorsey Bigbury on the Mendips, the Stripple Stones in Cornwall, Arbor Low in Derbyshire, and even as far afield as Stennis in Orkney; of these only the first is known to have been built by the Beaker-Folk, but the probability is that they had some share in the inspiration of them all, and the raising of these temples throughout Britain is further proof of the widespread religious conformity that this people was able to impose. Their orthodoxy, however, inevitably became less in regions remote from their main settlements, as is shown by their actual use of the old Megalithic collective tombs in the Scottish Isles and their adaptation of a passage-grave tradition in the remarkable 'Recumbent Stone' circles of north-east Scotland. In these the stone uprights regularly increase in size towards one side, where the tallest pair flank a massive recumbent slab, in one instance as much as 17 feet long. They were not intended to serve wholly, or perhaps even primarily, as temples, but enclosed cremated burials under a small central cairn, sometimes furnished with a passage and kerb, all reminiscent of passage-grave traditions.

Those who are familiar with the moorlands of Cornwall, Somerset, Wales, and the north of England will have seen simple circles of standing stones ranging in diameter from less than 50 to over 300 feet. Often it is not known when these were set up or by whom; some may be much later than Beaker times, but they should all fall within the limits of the Bronze Age. Perhaps the most fascinating thing about them is their names – Long Meg, the Nine and the Merry Maidens, the Hurlers and the Weddings, to quote a few – and the attendant folklore which tells how they are men and girls petrified for dancing and playing on the Sabbath, or wedding-parties and invading armies similarly turned to stone, and how they may return to life under the cover of darkness to dance again or drink at a nearby stream.

Before leaving the Early Bronze Age we can revert for a moment to purely secular matters. The ignorance of domestic life in this period which we have regretted in the case of the nomadic Beaker Folk is to some extent made good by the happy survival of an entire hamlet of the same age in the Orkneys. Its inhabitants were not themselves of true Beaker stock, but had probably been forced to quit the Continent to make way before the Beaker expansion. Kinsfolk of theirs were settled in many parts of Britain, particularly on the East coast, where they probably first landed, and in Wessex, but it so happens that it is only in the remote Orkneys that we can get any clear idea of their way of life. Here the most complete and best known of their settlements is Skara Brae, a village whose final fate was to be overwhelmed with drifting sand – sand which has preserved it from decay for thousands of years. In the teeth of a harsh and inhospitable climate, a hardy group of colonists found it possible to form a settled community supported by herds of cows and sheep pastured on the open grassland, and by an abundant supply of shell-fish. Together these provided a staple diet which they could vary with venison, sea-birds and fish, although no trouble was taken to devise specialized implements for hunting or fishing.

Agriculture was not practised at all. They used no metal or foreign raw materials of any kind, and were as entirely self-supporting as any Neolithic community: an independent, intimate society, often cut off from the world by gales and rough seas, and concerned with little beyond the struggle for its own existence. As in such conditions there was no need for warfare, Skara Brae economy was quite free from the burden of armaments, and if life was hard, it was peaceful. The half-dozen houses and communal workshop were huddled together for mutual warmth and shelter, the narrow alleyways between being roofed, and the whole cluster served by an efficient sewerage system of slab-lined drains.

A house consisted of a single, well-sized living-room with corbelled roof and one or more side cells that probably served as storerooms and privies. It is astonishingly good fortune to find in Britain houses largely intact after some 3500 years, but yet more fortunate that they should still contain much of their original furnishings (Pl. 6). Wood being almost unobtainable on these windswept islands, the villagers instead used the local flagstone to build furniture that was not only convenient but imperishable. So it is that we can reconstruct complete domestic interiors and sense something of their atmosphere. And they must have been pleasant enough homes. Imagine with what relief a woman returning in the early dusk of a northern winter afternoon, perhaps with hands cold and aching after collecting shell-fish, would have turned into the comparative shelter of the village alleys. Exchanging a word with a neighbour, she would duck through the low entrance of her hut until she could stand upright below her own roof and enjoy the warmth and familiar fragrance of the peat. Putting her limpets in a richly decorated pot on the stone dresser, she could sit on the edge of one of the two box-beds, with their mattresses of heather and skins, and warm her hands at the central fire. Above the bed behind her head a recess let into the wall would contain her special possessions, while opposite the store-room was readily accessible through a low doorway. Altogether nearly as well-equipped and comfortable a dwelling as many inhabited in such remote regions up to the last century. But the element of savagery was there, and one instance would not be far to seek: hidden in the foundations were the crouched bodies of two old women, buried that their spirits might hold up the walls of the house.

Towards the end of the long life of the Skara Brae village a few Beaker Folk crossed to the Orkneys in the most northerly wavelet of the great tide of their invasion of Britain. This tide had swept over the whole country, inundating the Neo-lithic escape, but now it began to subside and some of the old landmarks to reappear, although largely transformed as a result of their submergence. The invaders had made a great contribution to the age that was to follow, but as time went by and they became assimilated with the remains of the old population, their culture lost its narrow identity. Further-more, the cultural uniformity which their forceful overlord-ship had imposed broke down, and we find that at this point, the end of the Early and the beginning of the Middle Bronze Age, Britain is divided into two provinces, each with its own history. While north of the Thames valley the various racial elements that went to make up the Early Bronze Age population were left to intermarry, fuse and develop their blended culture uninterrupted, south of it this process was given a different complexion by a fresh invasion of Wessex from the Continent.

In the northern province the Peterborough race reappears, stiffened by a strong Beaker element and with a valuable inheritance from the metallurgical and commercial interests of the passage-grave people (p. 61). The product of this mingling of races and their traditions was a distinctively British growth awkwardly named the Food-Vessel culture. The Food-Vessel province can itself be subdivided into an Irish and south-west Scottish and a north-west British region with slightly divergent lines of development.

The habits of life which had come down to them both from their Peterborough and Beaker ancestors inclined the Food-Vessel people to a nomadic existence, winning their food supplies by stock-raising and hunting, while agriculture declined yet further in importance. But commerce certainly had its place in their economy, and prompted many of them to settle along the natural trade routes of Scotland and northern England, some of which had first been opened by the passage-grave people. Here they acted as middlemen and distributors between the Irish bronze- and gold-smiths and their customers in Britain and northern Europe, while the familiar Atlantic route from Ireland carried the same goods to western France and Iberia. Ireland was becoming one of the chief mining and industrial centres of Early Bronze-Age Europe, and the Food-Vessel traders drew their share of the profits. So successful were they that they were able to deck themselves, and more especially their women-folk, with a variety of ostentatious ornaments. How many wealthy merchants since then have used the bosoms of their wives and daughters to display before the eyes of the world bright tokens of their own success! The height of fashion for

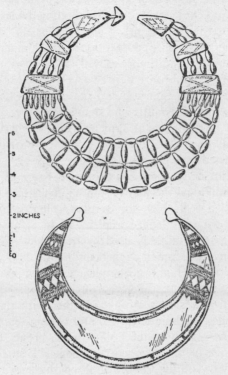

FIG. 7. Jet bead-necklace and gold 'lunula'
of the Early Bronze Age.

Food-Vessel women were elaborate necklets of Yorkshire jet, crescentic in shape and built up from a number of ingeniously threaded beads and engraved plaques (Fig. 7, top). Never again until Victorian ladies jangled with a host of lockets, beads, brooches and bracelets were our native diamonds to enjoy such a vogue.

In Ireland this necklace was rendered in a still more sumptuous medium – a sheet-gold necklet of the same crescentic shape, and chased with designs imitating the layout of the jet plaques (Fig. 7, bottom). Such necklets, known to the pedantic as *lunulae*, were exported to Denmark, northwestern Germany and France as well as to the British market. Earrings of gold or bronze were also worn, of a sophisticated, basket-like pattern that was perhaps originally designed by Mediterranean goldsmiths who shaped similar rings to hang in the ears of the ladies of Troy and Egypt. Men as well as women may have worn the torques made from simple gold ribbon twisted into glittering spirals.

Stone still served for many tools and weapons, of which the most individual was an oval flint knife flaked all over one surface with a skill which proves that fine flint-knapping was not yet a lost art. Bronze implements at first show little advance on those already used by the Beaker Folk, being limited to flat axes, small daggers and halberds.

Potting was not highly accomplished. The women seem to have inherited from their Peterborough forebears an inability to fire their wares successfully, together with their rather clumsy 'coiled' technique (p. 66) and certain features from their designs – such as the hollow neck, broad, decorated rim, and love of unrestrained ornament (Pl. 3B). This was particularly true in the Food-Vessel region centred in northeastern England; in Ireland a lighter and more rounded form of bowl was usual, whose superior craftsmanship may have been due to knowledge handed down from the megalithic culture of the west.

Religious doctrine too may have drawn largely on megalithic religion, and they employed a symbolism that is only a further simplification and stylization of that shown in passage-grave art (p. 62). This is manifest also in the most famous and curious cult objects of the time, the chalk-cut idols that were found under a round barrow at Folkton in eastern Yorkshire (Fig. 8). These squat, drum-shaped idols

FIG. 8. Drum-shaped chalk idol of the Early Bronze Age, from a barrow at Folkton, Yorks.

are carved with eye symbols and owl faces that would certainly have been understood by the megalithic people of Iberia and the western Mediterranean many centuries before. Yet there is little trace of megalithic ideas in the burial customs of the Food-Vessel societies. The dead were most often buried much as the Beaker Folk had been, the bodies lying crouched under round barrows or cairns; although there might be several graves under one mound, they were essentially individual, and there is no implication of a communal rite. Another most interesting although less frequent practice was that of placing the corpse in a coffin hollowed out from an oak-trunk and sometimes shaped to resemble a boat. Here we have a reflection of the Egyptian idea of a passage by water to the next world, an idea which took firm root at this time also in Scandinavia, where it was to flower

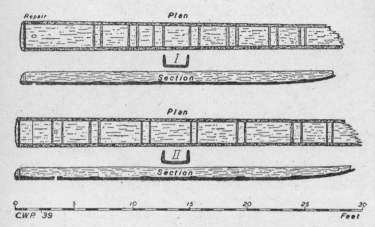

FIG. 9. Dug-out canoes of the Bronze Age,
from the Trent at Wilford, Notts.

at last in the magnificent ship-burials of the Vikings. This conception would not be alien to the Food-Vessel people, many of whom must have been habitual sailors adept at driving their dug-outs far overseas on their distant trading ventures. It must have been a man with such experiences behind him who was buried under the great cairn at Loose Howe in Yorkshire lying in a ritual boat (similar to Fig. 9) covered by another inverted and with a smaller one riding like a dinghy by his side.

In addition to the food vessel itself, stone and occasionally metal implements and ornaments, including jet necklaces, were interred with the dead. One cannot but reflect on the emotions of a young woman of the day when she had to watch some coveted and perhaps irreplaceable ornament despatched to the next world with her grandmother.

While the Food-Vessel people were left to develop their culture and commerce in undisturbed possession of the country north of the Thames, Wessex was the scene of more dramatic events. The population there was a very similar ethnic hotch-potch of Beaker Folk and surviving Neolithic strains, but the process of their fusion and development was to be modified from without. In about 1450 B.C., once again, as at the opening of the Early Bronze Age, boats were crossing the Channel from Brittany bringing parties of well-armed warriors to annex the ever-desirable Wessex uplands. They were relatively few in number, but they succeeded in establishing a suzerainty over the native inhabitants, availing themselves of their labour, their wealth and their wives. Thus the descendants of the Beaker conquerors had to suffer the same fate that they had themselves meted out to the Neolithic peasantry a few generations earlier. With the essentials of life so easily provided, this new aristocracy was able to afford possessions far more varied and extravagant than anything known in Britain before. For their pleasure luxury goods were carried over great distances and from many quarters – the range of their trade connexions outstretched even those of the Food-Vessel people. Amber was brought from the Baltic, ornaments from central Europe, gold and bronze from Ireland, faience beads from Egypt. These gay blue beads were the first actual products of any Eastern civilization known to have reached this country, apparently through middlemen in the Aegean and Central Europe, and it is not until the days of the Roman Empire 1500 years later that we know of any others. The fact that they could be imported in considerable numbers is, then, sufficient proof of the exceptional power and organization of the Wessex chieftains. Nor was Egypt the only civilized land with which they had contacts. Many details of design and technique in Wessex ornaments and weapons show that they were influenced by the craftsmanship of Greece, where the magnificent Mycenean civilization was now at its height. The ribbed gold cup (Pl. 5A) from Rillaton in Cornwall recalls one from a rich grave at Mycenae itself, while one of the Cretan merchant princes ruling over the brilliant court of Knossos did not despise a gold-bound amber disc almost identical with pendants worn by his contemporaries in Wiltshire.

One of the advantages which secured the power of the new rulers was a greatly superior armament. They had daggers strengthened with a stout midrib and large enough to be formidable, and axes with flanged sides that at once increased their rigidity and allowed their hafting to be much more secure. These new forms not only outclassed the old flat daggers and axes in effectiveness, their manufacture demanded a far more advanced technique of bronze-founding that opened the way for future development. The simple, flat, open mould would no longer suffice. For these shapes with relief on two faces a double mould filled through a gate was necessary.

Such new methods imply the presence of new men. The Wessex chiefs must have brought with them from Brittany a few skilled bronze-smiths, practised in double-mould casting and furnished with a repertory of designs that was ultimately drawn from central Europe. Smiths schooled in the Irish traditions, if their goods were not to be driven from the best markets, had soon to imitate the improved designs and

methods of the newcomers, and the old inefficient implements fell out of use except in Ireland and the remote regions
of northern Scotland. From this pooling of native and foreign
talent grew the great British school of metallurgy that was to
produce such excellent and individual work during the ensuing
centuries of the Middle Bronze Age (p. 98). The Wessex chieftains also wielded heavy spherical stone maces, and used
arrows tipped with exquisitely finished flint heads – long and
narrow, with neatly squared, straight barbs quite unlike
those of the Beaker Folk.

A fully caparisoned warrior must have made quite a
splendid figure. Imagine as an example the tall, stalwart man
who came to be buried under the Bush Barrow at Normanton
in Wiltshire. He possessed an axe, and two massive daggers,
one of which had a hilt sparkling with an intricate gold inlay
and was hooked to his belt from a finely chased gold plate.
Two other gold plates enriched his dress, and as a badge of
rank he carried a curious sceptre with a stone head and
elaborately cut bone mounts. Such sceptres suggest a truly
princely pomp. Alike in meaning and in form, they are in
line with their modern descendants, the ceremonial maces
and other baubles that so often embarrass the actors in our
present-day rituals.

All manner of ornaments were fashionable besides the
amber discs, faience beads and gold plaques already described. Beads might be made of gold, amber or shale, and
sometimes necklaces were hung with pendants in the shape
of miniature halberds that evidently had some symbolic
significance. The women wore necklets identical with the jet
crescents of their Food-Vessel contemporaries, but made
instead from a foreign substance, amber. Amber had a strange
importance in prehistoric Europe. Not only was it decorative, but the ease with which it became electrified gave it

magical powers that had an appeal even for the sophisticated societies of the Mediterranean. The Baltic was almost the sole source of this precious resin, which had lain there ever since it was exuded by the great conifer forests of far earlier times. The trade routes that carried it right across Europe, over the Alpine passes and down to the Aegean, were the main channels along which ideas from the Eastern civilizations could flow to the benighted peoples of the north-west. Amber was a potent instrument for the diffusion of culture. Among its largest purchasers were the Wessex aristocrats, who imparted the raw material in bulk. Not content with small ornaments, they even had it carved into handled cups that were presumably reserved for ritual use. Similar cups were turned from shale (and no doubt also in wood), and to do work of this kind trained artisans must have been employed, just as bronze-smiths were needed as armourers. Among them would have been specialists in beating and engraving gold, in cutting amber and in turning shale – living either as independent itinerants, or as camp-followers attached to the persons of the chiefs. An aristocracy, priests perhaps, a mixed peasantry, traders, miners, smiths and other artisans: society was becoming more complex.

In their burial customs the Wessex rulers followed the round-barrow tradition first introduced into Britain by the Beaker Folk, and now widespread on the Continent. They favoured in particular two new forms of round tumulus. Among the simple 'bowl' barrows which stud the southern chalk one can often pick out a variety in which the central mound is separated by a level shelf or platform from its surrounding ditch. This is the so-called 'bell' barrow (Pl. 2c), a form of tomb which covers many of the richest chieftains' graves. In the second variety, the still more distinctive 'disc' barrow, the mound has shrunk to a mere anthill in size, ringed by a circular ditch and bank which have become the conspicuous features. Both types of monument are usually cut from the chalk with masterly precision and finish, and may be picked out in the air photograph Pl. 7.

Bodies were still sometimes inhumed, but now for the first time cremation was the prevalent rite in southern England. The remains, whether burnt or unburnt, were contained in a wooden coffin or laid on a plank floor, and with them went the dead man's ornaments, weapons and tools in ungrudging abundance. Specially designed funerary pottery was also used. The most interesting and charming are tiny ritual vessels, ornamented in a variety of ways, that were novelties introduced by the invaders. Large urns like Pl. 5B, on the other hand, were designed by the women of the subject population, who incorporated in them memories of beaker and Peterborough wares.

The disc and bell barrows crowd round Stonehenge and Avebury in numbers which prove the continued sanctity of these great temples, and we have seen that the remodelling of Stonehenge into something like its present form was apparently ordained by the lords of the Wessex culture.

The heyday of the Wessex culture, together with the Food-Vessel period of the north, is recognized as forming the second half of our Early Bronze Age. But in fact the Wessex invasion might almost equally well be said to initiate the Middle Bronze Age. Certainly one period runs imperceptibly into the next with an unbroken continuity of culture. The full Middle Bronze Age is distinguished not by anything new, but by the gradual self-assertion and expansion of the native elements in the population.

Known as the Urn people, from the large cineraries which the women made for funerary use (above), they began this expansion in about 1400 B.C., and pushed on slowly but relentlessly during the ensuing centuries of the Middle Bronze Age. At last their range was even wider than that of the Beaker Folk before them, for they not only crossed from Scotland to Ulster and effectively colonized the greater part of Ireland, but also settled regions in England such as north-east Yorkshire, Cheshire and the Pennines, which had hitherto been shunned for the poverty of their soil. A pastoral people themselves, they had no difficulty in mingling with the Food-Vessel societies, of whom they were, moreover, close blood relations (p. 85). So it was not by force of arms, but by peaceful penetration and absorption that they succeeded in dominating their new territories. But dominate they did: gradually the Food-Vessel culture gave way before them, though not without adding to the common inheritance.

Although their main food supplies came from their flocks and the hunting of wild game, the Urn people practised agriculture, probably still simple hoe cultivation by the womenfolk. They even grew a new grain, barley, side by side with the wheats that had been known since Neolithic times. Some of the earliest surviving fields to be seen in Britain were probably first tilled by them – some small, irregular plots that survive on Dartmoor and the Cleveland Hills. On Dartmoor it is easy to detect how the women, as they turned the shallow soil with their hoes, gathered into heaps or threw to the edges of their plots the stones with which they were cluttered. Their homes stood near by, on the sites now marked by 'hut circles', groups of round stone houses with clustering beehive roofs, sometimes, as at Grimspound, ringed by a protective wall. Peat smoke drifting from the roofs and through the stone-lintelled doorways would come from a central fire like those which had burned a few centuries earlier far to the north at Skara Brae.

Plate 1A : The Chambered Tomb of Bryn Celli Ddu, Anglesey.   Entrance.

Plate 1B : The Chambered Tomb of New Grange, Ireland : carving at the entrance.

Plate 2A: A typical Long Barrow (Therfield Heath, Royston).

Plate 2B: An Early Bronze Age burial (Snailwell, near Newmarket).

Plate 2C: A typical Round Barrow, of the "bell" type (Normanton, near Stonehenge).

Plate 3A : A pottery Beaker of the
Early Stone Age.

Plate 3B : A pottery Food-vessel of the
Early Bronze Age. Diameter $7\frac{1}{2}$ ins.

Plate 4A: Avebury

Plate 4B: Stonehenge: some of the trilithons.

INCHES

Plate 5A: Gold Cup of the Bronze Age,
from a grave at Rillaton, Cornwall.

Plate 5B: Pottery Cinerary Urn of the
Middle Bronze Age (Tyringham,
Bucks).

INCHES

Plate 6: Skara Brae, Orkney: a house in the Late Neolithic village (of early Bronze-Age date).

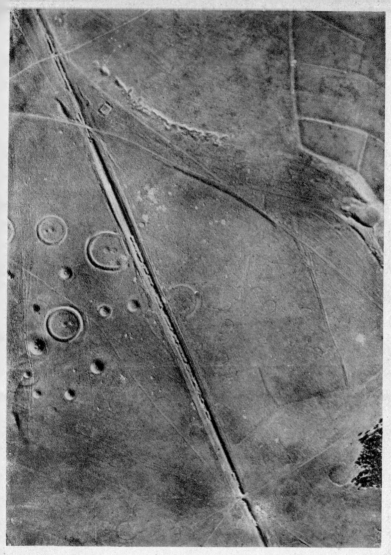

Plate 7: Bronze Age Round Barrows from the air (Oakley Down, Dorset). Below, Celtic fields; across the middle, a Roman road.

Plate 8: Celtic Fields on Fyfield Down, Wiltshire, from the air.

Plate 9: The Witham Sword. Scale, ⅔. (Of iron, with bronze scabbard-ornament).

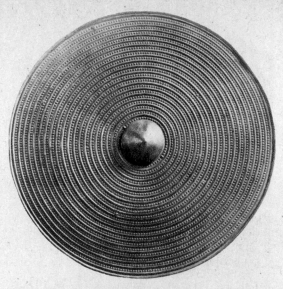

Plate 10A: Bronze Shield of the Late Bronze Age, from Carnarvonshire. Diameter 25 ins.

Plate 10B: Gold Peytrel of the Late Bronze Age, from Mold, Flintshire.

Plate 11A: Bronze figure of a boar, from Hounslow. Length just over 2 ins.

Plate 11B: Enamelled bronze harness-mount, from Polden Hill, Somerset. Scale, about ⅔.

Plate 12: Celtic craftsmanship in bronze: detail of an altar-top or dish from Ireland. Scale, about ¾.

Plate 13: The Battersea Shield (of bronze, with red
enamel in the studs).   Scale, about ⅛.

Plate 14: Maiden Castle, Dorset: the ramparts from the air.

Plate 15: Uffington Castle, Berks, and the White Horse, from the air.

Plate 16A: Wrought-iron firedog, from Lord's Bridge, Cambridgeshire, with terminals in the form of ox-heads. Scale, about $\frac{1}{12}$.

Plate 16B: Bronze bridle-bit, from Polden Hill, Somerset. Scale, about $\frac{1}{3}$.

Houses and fields have survived on Dartmoor only because the stony soil has saved it from the plough: settlements of the Urn people on more fertile lands certainly existed, but have been obliterated by long ages of cultivation. Here and there, most notably in the Thames valley, the acute eyes of air observers and their cameras have detected and recorded the ghostly outlines of ring ditches, some of which may have enclosed groups of light huts or tents. And at Rams Hill on the Berkshire Downs is a ditched counterpart of the stone-walled steadings of the moors.

As well as grain, the women raised crops of flax for linen, while the wool from their sheep they wove into materials that were sometimes of extraordinary fineness. Such fabrics were, of course, intended for clothes, and now for the first time we have a notion of prevalent fashions. No garments worn by British Urnfolk have survived, but a great deal is known of contemporary Danish costume, and dress on either side of the North Sea may well have had something in common. In Denmark oak coffins lying in waterlogged barrows have preserved for us suits of clothes complete in every detail. Men wore round woollen caps that must have been jauntily becoming, long cloaks hanging in full, graceful folds from their shoulders, and knee-length kirtles held up with woollen girdles. The women also had cloaks, but under them fashion demanded short-sleeved jackets, and skirts that could either be of woven cloth, long and formal, or a mere corded fringe just covering the knees. One lady increased the apparent abundance of her hair, which was of true Nordic fairness, by a concealed pad. The resulting bun was held in a net of intricately woven horsehair remarkably like the nets so fashionable in Victorian days and now enjoying a revival in the 1940's.

As for ornaments to enliven such clothes, the Urn people

could not generally afford the lavish display of the Wessex chiefs. Nevertheless they did contrive to secure faience beads, and some of the leading families, those who by fair means or foul owned the most head of cattle and sheep, were probably able to buy some of the wonderful gold work which is the pride of the Irish Middle Bronze Age. Most striking and opulent were the great torques made from four-flanged rods of gold twisted into glistening spirals and fastening with massive terminal hooks. These were traded not only to many parts of England, but by way of the south-western peninsula to Brittany and the Channel Isles. The most dramatic discovery was made at Grunty Fen in Cambridgeshire, when a peat-cutter, on removing a turf, saw something like a golden snake rise up from the dark soil. This was a torque which had been coiled up and buried for safety in some time of trouble well over 3000 years before.

With bronze implements the Urn people became increasingly well equipped. As the centuries passed undisturbed by foreign conquest, the British smiths used a body of skill and knowledge based on the old Irish traditions, but fertilized by the Continental ideas of the Wessex invaders, to create a very successful native school of metallurgy.

Starting with the dagger and the flanged axe, they gradually adapted them to meet fresh needs. To follow the history of these technical developments archaeology resorts to one of its favourite methods, the typological study, which in this context means no more than arranging in their due order the various stages by which the groping craftsman makes an article more efficient, and perhaps at the same time more beautiful, or allows it to degenerate, and perhaps to become uglier. It is the same simple method which we all use instinctively when judging by eye the date of a motor-car, a wireless set or a tail-coat. Many people will still be able to recollect

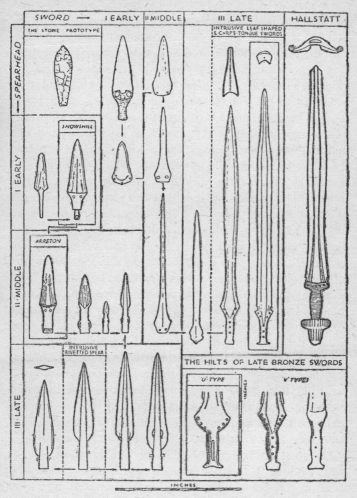

FIG. 10. The development of the Bronze Age dagger,
spearhead and sword.

the evolution of the modern double-decker bus with internal stairs from the old horse-bus with outside steps. In prehistoric times there are few more perfect sequences of this kind than that leading from the dagger to the socketed spear (Fig. 10). First a long tang was added to secure the dagger blade into the shaft of a spear, then a ferrule was found to be necessary to prevent the shaft from splitting, next it was thought better to make blade, ferrule and tang in one piece, finally the central tang was seen to be superfluous and was omitted, while loops were added to hold thongs for binding the head to the shaft. This process, which took place in the earlier years of the Middle Bronze Age, ended with a thoroughly serviceable weapon that also had a simple strength of line most agreeable to the eye. He would be an austere functionalist indeed who could object to the useless but pleasing pair of raised knobs on the socket imitating the rivet-heads which in an earlier stage had served to secure the ferrule. On the other hand when, later, the leaf-shaped form of blade came in, the side loops were moved up the socket into contact with its base; and when they became mere 'ornamental' openings in the wings of the blade, one should perhaps admit degeneration. This long story of the British socketed spear shows clearly how the typological method depends on man's natural conservatism, which prevents him from making any abrupt break with past forms – the same unchanging conservatism which to-day keeps a useless and labour-making row of buttons on the cuffs of his coat. Without it archaeology would often be at a loss.

The other new forms evolved at this time have less complicated histories. It is easy to see how a gradual increase in the length of the blade accompanied by a strengthening of the midrib would convert the dagger into the rapier of Fig. 10, sometimes as much as 20–30 inches long, and an elegant

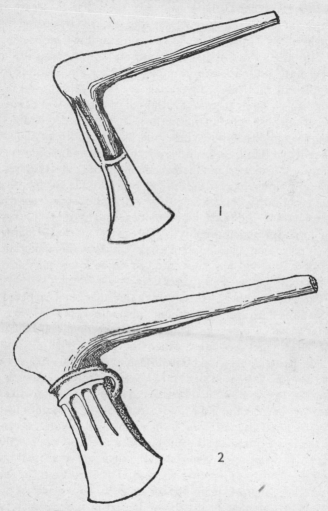

FIG. 11. Hafted bronze axes of the Middle and
Late Bronze Ages.

weapon well adapted for sticking a man in the ribs. With the axe the problem to be solved was how best to secure it between the forks of its haft; this was achieved by raising the height of the flanges to prevent any up-and-down movement, and adding a ridge across the centre to hold the ends of the fork, and so stop the axe from pushing back and splitting its handle. In the fully evolved palstave (Fig. 11, bottom) the problem was well answered, although in form it was always rather uncouth, lacking the fine lines of spearhead and rapier. For what purpose were these offensive weapons intended? They may often have been used in hunting, and the axe had many practical uses, but there seems little doubt that they were primarily intended for fighting. As the Middle Bronze Age was a period singularly free from external dangers, one can assume that the Urn communities fought one another, for territory and for booty – more particularly for cattle. Even so soon do we find man's most precious raw materials, greatest skill and most advanced scientific knowledge dedicated to killing his own species.

Once dead, either by this means or another, the Urn people were almost invariably cremated, the bodies being burned on great pyres of oak logs. Their ashes were then collected in the large cineraries after which they are named (Pl. 5B). These great, clumsy and often ill-fashioned jars are in a sense an enlarged variant of the Food Vessel adapted for funerary use. The urns were sometimes ranged in cemeteries, but much more frequently the old round-barrow usage was continued, the principal cremation often in a central cist with the urns of the less distinguished dead buried round it. Occasionally the barrow has been piled round the structure of a ritual hut in a manner reminiscent of the earlier Beaker Folk (p. 75). For other funerals, again, the sanctuary of holy places of the past was sought, the urns being buried in the precincts of stone circles or megalithic tombs. One most remarkable site which must have been a shrine in honour of two illustrious individuals is at Bleasdale in Lancashire, where a pair of cremation urns in a central pit were surrounded by a ring of massive oak posts, a ditch with an entrance causeway, and a large outer circle of posts linked with palisading.

Doctrine concerned with an after life changed considerably in the Middle Bronze Age. The regular adoption of crema-tion is evidence for a less concrete conception of the fate of the physical body, a conception which is again implied by a very great simplification in the equipping of the dead. For the Urn burials are never accompanied by an elaborate dis-play of weapons and ornaments such as went into the earth with the Wessex chiefs and the wealthier of the Beaker Folk. The gold torques, axes, spears and rapiers are never found in graves. A poor knife, a few beads, bone pins and belt-fasteners, occasionally a bronze razor that had probably served some ritual purpose, are the most that was left with the ashes. Evidently it was no longer considered necessary that a man should go into the next world in full pride of his earthly possessions.

This chapter has treated a stretch of British prehistory which has been conventionally and not inconveniently divi-ded into two parts, the Early and the Middle Bronze Ages. But we have found these Ages to be so closely interlocked that the division is all but arbitrary. It is, in fact, more realis-tic to see the Bronze Age as opening with a time of movement, change and diversity which passes into one of slow settling-down, assimilation and uniformity. The first is a phase of impact on Britain from the Continent: the several invasions of the Skara Brae and Beaker peoples, followed rapidly in the south by the influx of the Wessex warriors. Then comes the calmer period after about 1400 B.C., when the various stocks old and new which had by then established themselves in the country united their blood and their traditions until, as the Urn people, they were able to spread an almost uniform culture throughout the British Isles. And this culture had time to grow insular, to develop a more distinctively British flavour than that of any previous prehistoric age. Undisturbed in these islands, the Urn communities had little concern with what went on across the sea. But, one wonders, did traders ever bring them news? Did they learn of the fall of the ancient and wealthy court of Knossos, destroyed in about 1400 B.C., probably by the Myceneans of mainland Greece? That all-important event, symbolized in Greek myth by the slaying of the Minotaur, can be said to mark the liberation of European civilization from its long dependence on the Orient. Or a generation later did they hear tell of the strange revolution led by the mystical young Egyptian pharaoh Akhenaten? How he built an entire new city where he could worship the one true god, paint, and dally with his lovely Nefertiti? That was a world far removed in spirit from the contemporary British scene, where a pastoral society was preoccupied with matters of stock-raising, hunting and inter-tribal feuds. They had little in common but the memory of a few blue beads. Perhaps the Urn people would have asked nothing more than to be allowed to forget the existence of all lands beyond the Channel except for the purposes of a little quiet trade. But the Continent was inexorably there, and was rousing from its Middle Bronze Age quiescence.

CHAPTER IV

The Late Bronze Age

THE date 900 B.C., when (roughly) the British Late Bronze Age opens, is a good one at which to reflect on the racial pattern which was emerging on the Continent. For we are now on the edge of historic times. Soon it will begin to be possible to recognize people under their proper names. It is not always easy to remember that the very peoples whom we have met under the odd-sounding titles invented for them by archaeology, after the birth and death of a few generations will emerge into the lighted strip of history bearing such familiar titles as Celts, Germans and Illyrians. The difficulty is to know how far back into prehistory we can legitimately push these identifications: how early, for instance, speak of Celts, when be more cautious with proto-Celts, and when the distance in time becomes too great for any name to be safely applied.

The broadest racial divisions of Europe have already been suggested in earlier chapters, and may be said to have held good from Neolithic times to the present day. These are the small, dark Mediterraneans in the south, the sturdy, round-headed Alpines along the mountain lands from the Balkans to Spain, and the tall, fair Nordics. But recognition of those subtle divisions, which are rather a question of common language and culture than of identity of blood, is much more difficult. As the Late Bronze and Iron Ages in western Europe are largely dominated by the Celts, one must ask 'Who were the Celts?' When they first began to play a part in history they are a people in process of expanding in many directions from their homelands in France and western

Germany. And we know that the inhabitants of this region must have been largely descended from a mixture of Battle-Axe warriors, who were predominantly Nordic, and round-headed Beaker Folk from the south, on a solid substratum of Neolithic and ultimately Mesolithic stocks; in fact, very much the same mixture which composed the Middle Bronze Age Urn societies in Britain. We need not doubt that the language these Urn people spoke as they drove their flocks and hunted their game from end to end of these islands must have been already recognizably Celtic.

But the Celticization of Britain was to be continued or intensified by a series of fresh invasions during the 900 years covered by the Late Bronze and Iron Ages. These were caused by the expansion of two great Continental peoples. Away to the north of the Celtic lands Germanic tribes were breeding with their customary fecundity, while to the east of them, in central Europe, was a virile people of Illyrian stock, hardly less prolific. Almost simultaneously they began the drive for more living space, the Germans crossing the Elbe and ulti-mately thrusting down towards Holland, the Illyrians pushing westward until the effects of their pressure were felt across France as far as the Channel coasts. It was the Celtic tribes who had to absorb or give way before the impact of these western migrations. And Britain, as ever, stood open as a sanctuary for the victims of Continental upheaval.

After 900, probably nearer 800 B.C., a few small groups of Celts began their infiltration: some may have gone from north-west Germany to northern England and perhaps even on to Ireland, while others crossed from northern France to the Kent and Sussex coasts.

One such party of refugees, probably representative of many others, established a farm in a lovely position on the South Downs, on Plumpton Plain, near Brighton. Here they made themselves a settled homestead, where they lived in round, thatched huts standing within earthen banks, linked by tracks with the cattle enclosures that lay near by. Round about the farm stretched a number of small, squarish corn-fields, among the first of their kind to be tilled on British soil (p. 112). This little refugee community was evidently largely independent of the Urn people among whom it was planted, and maintained many of its Continental ways – the women, for instance, made much the same handled and incised pots which they had shaped from the clay of northern France. This was probably true of most of the colonists who reached Britain during this opening phase of the Late Bronze Age: they made little impression on the Urn com-munities, whose mainly pastoral and hunting life went on as before.

But already before their coming we can see the great develop-ment which distinguishes the beginning of the Late from the end of the Middle Bronze Age – a sudden adoption of many new bronze implements and a revolutionary change in the methods of the bronze industry itself. The metal was now becoming obtainable in larger and larger quantities as organization of the mining and transport of copper and tin improved. At the same time, the founders grew increasingly inventive, and devised ingenious new techniques in casting which allowed them to speed up their output and elaborate their designs. The bronze-founders present an interesting social phenomenon. They formed themselves into a wealthy class almost independent of established society, a caste of itinerants who ranged wide regions in pursuit of markets. It seems that there were no middlemen, these travelling smiths themselves making the implements they sold. They acted also as scrap-metal merchants, buying up their customers' broken or old-fashioned bronzes, probably taking them in part exchange for new types fresh from their own methods.

Travellers in little-civilized lands are always liable to meet accidents, occasionally sudden death, so it is not surprising that throughout Europe and the British Isles the contents of the bronze-smiths' workbags are found to-day in many places where they have lain since they were lost in bogs, or from capsized boats, or were buried in an emergency and never reclaimed. Such collections usually include not only finished implements, but also solid lumps of metal that have been melted down in crucibles, odds and ends of scrap, and sometimes quantities of old implements fused together into a strange, distorted mass in preparation for melting and recasting.

Merchants who traded overseas brought the Urn people new ideas for the design of implements that had been thought out on the Continent. They could offer an axe with a wide socket which avoided the weak point always present in the forked haft of the older palstave (Fig. 11, bottom). Yet the latter remained in use throughout the period, perhaps because the weight in its solid blade made it more effective for hard cutting than the light socketed form. They also brought a laurel-leaf-shaped spearhead which was pegged or tied to its haft through a pair of holes in the socket. These were efficient enough weapons, but they always suffer from a cheap, mass-produced look, and have little of the beauty of line of the native side-looped spear. A much more significant new weapon which the itinerants could put into the hands of the Urn men was a fine double-edged sword (Fig. 10), usually fitted with a leather scabbard ending in a long, tongue-shaped chape. Such swords differ from the older rapier which they displaced in being designed for slashing as well as stabbing blows. The changed manner of fighting which this design implies may well have imitated the practice of the refugees (p. 106), who would have been familiar with it in their Continental homes.

Another change for which these refugees were responsible concerns not fighting, but clothing. Whereas since Early Bronze Age times the people of Britain had generally followed the Mediterranean habit of buttoning themselves into their clothes, they now began to share the north European preference for large pins, a considerable variety of which were in fashion at this time.

Although these many new bronze forms were Continental in origin, like all foreign intrusions they soon assumed a distinctive British character. Native British craftsmen adapted the designs, and, backed by their good supplies of raw material from Cornwall and Ireland, were soon themselves exporting largely to the Continent, most freely to northern France.

In this way passed the first two centuries of our Late Bronze Age. While Greece was leaving the dark age following on the Trojan War, and was about to draw the first breath of classical civilization with the production of her austere archaic sculpture, and while Italy was cradling the strange Etruscan culture, we have seen that the pastoral Urn societies which had dominated Britain in the Middle Bronze Age continued much as before. They did little more than take full advantage of the improved equipment that was now on the market, and accept in their midst a few foreign refugees and merchants.

But in southern and south-east England their long period of undisturbed dominion was at last to be ended. The straggling immigrants of this first phase were the precursors of much more substantial Celtic invasions that began in the middle of the eighth century B.C. In the coming era the

Continent was again and again to overflow on to our shores. Already in the eighth century the picture is sufficiently complicated. If some privileged being endowed with more than normal vision, exceptional patience and a long life could have watched from a lofty peak in the centre of England, he would have had to witness wave after wave of immigrants disembarking along the east and south coasts from Yorkshire to Land's End. Straining his eyes towards the Continent for an explanation of this exodus, he could see that its prime cause was the continued land-hunger of the Illyrian peoples, who had by now given something of their culture and race to the Celtic inhabitants of much of south and west Germany, parts of France and the western Alps. He could watch their pressure westwards expelling many of the inhabitants of Holland from their old territories, until, taking to their boats, they crossed the North Sea to our eastern coast.

Meanwhile, a scrutiny of the western Alps would show him a more dramatic scene. There, securely housed on platforms rising on piles from the margins of some of the loveliest lakes in Europe, were prosperous communities not only practising sound mixed farming, but also masters of an extensive industry. They were turning out cheap bronze goods for export on a prodigious scale. Axes, spears, swords, sickles, bangles and a host of other objects useful and decorative came pouring from their foundries. But the observer would not fail to detect that their prosperity could not endure, for a wetter climate was turning the water which had been their best protection into an immediate danger – the lakes were creeping up and threatening to flood the stilted villages. And beyond he would suddenly notice an even greater, though human, threat. Warrior tribes of south Germany had learnt from Italy and the South the use of iron, and at last, after 700 B.C., armed with powerful iron swords, they came sweeping down to complete the distress of the unhappy lake-dwellers. But already he has been watching them leave their homes and come moving towards him, their cattle, sheep, pigs and dogs going with them. As they went, their advance had set other Celtic tribes of France in motion, and these, too, were thus now coming westward, crossing the Channel and sailing up our Wessex harbours, many of them using the excellent road into the interior afforded by the Stour-Avon estuaries at Christchurch. The French scene would show him movement from the Rhineland too, and a pressure of people from which some tribes were going northward over the narrow seas to settle in Sussex and Kent, to sail up the Thames estuary and spread north into East Anglia. Some of those who chose the Thames estuary found that along its muddy banks it was possible to set up pile dwellings very much like those which they had left behind in the strangely different surroundings of their Alpine homelands.

Thus the second half of the Late Bronze Age was certainly a time of many invasions, but as all the immigrants were racially akin, and akin also with the native Urn folk whom they found in possession, it was easy enough for them to settle down and form a nearly uniform culture throughout the English lowlands. Much of Yorkshire and the Highland zone they never penetrated; there the Urn communities were left to follow their pastoral pursuits for several centuries longer.

These Late Bronze Age invaders have been supplied with the euphonious but cumbersome title of Deverel-Rimbury people, a double-barrel formed from two of their burial sites in Dorset. Their methods of life were considerably influenced by the central European Illyric strain in their ancestry, most significantly in a very great increase in the importance of agriculture. This renewed emphasis on the raising of cereal crops was an event of deep and lasting importance in British history.

In any attempt to trace an ordered evolution in our social and economic life, periods will be encountered when there were setbacks in the main stream of development. The most familiar is that of the Dark Ages, when the growth of urban life initiated by the Romans was delayed for many centuries by the Anglo-Saxon invasions. It is true also in a much more limited sense of the Early and Middle Bronze Ages. The Windmill Hill people of the Neolithic Age belong more surely to the line of development that was to lead to the peasantry of medieval and later times than do the restless, warlike, pastoral peoples who were their immediate successors. With the coming of the Deverel-Rimbury tribes this interrupted agricultural evolution was resumed, and indeed received a sharp fillip. For they brought a new device which greatly increased the scope of cultivation. The hoe gave place to the plough, and the woman to the ox – or, more accurately, to a pair of oxen. Crop-raising was no longer to be a side-line, a small-scale tillage of garden plots, an activity that was more truly horticultural than agricultural. With the introduction of the two-ox, man-driven plough the importance of the harvest greatly increased, as corn began to be grown in regular field systems. The fields were still of modest size, in shape and area very like the small, stone-walled enclosures that are their modern descendants in Cornwall and many parts of Ireland, squarish in outline and rarely covering more than a quarter of an acre. This form of lay-out is known as the Celtic Field System, to distinguish it from the Strip System of long, narrow fields especially characteristic of Anglo-Saxon and medieval husbandry. It is not difficult to recapture an impression of our chalk country when it was covered with such little fields, for in many places their faint outlines still linger on the turf. On a ploughed slope the earth will tend to crop down towards the bottom of the field and pile up along the lower edge, until each field is separated from the one below by a slightly ridged step, while it is divided from its neighbours on either side by standing balks and the earth cast up by the turning of the plough. Banks formed in this way often show as a faint network spread on the slopes of chalk hills (Pl. 8), most clearly when picked out in shadow by a newly-risen or a setting sun.

The small size and rectangular shape of such fields was well suited to the light Mediterranean type of plough with which they were tilled, a coulterless implement which could not turn a sod, but merely scratch the surface with its short, straight share.

It would be quite false to suppose that all Deverel-Rimbury farmers were preoccupied exclusively with their crops. In many areas stock-breeding was no less important. But the old, nomadic, pastoral life was no longer suitable: communities were tied to the ploughlands in which so much labour was invested, and could no longer range freely over the open hills. Instead, pastures belonging to settled families or clans would have to be enclosed, and in many parts of the country, most conspicuously in Sussex, Hampshire, Dorset and on Salisbury Plain, it is still possible to trace the boundaries of many such enclosures or 'ranches'. They often lay on the northern slopes of hills whose sunnier aspects were reserved for cornfields, and each was enclosed by a chalk-cut ditch 5 feet deep, with a low bank on one or both sides. The white lines of these divisions must have gleamed conspicuously across the countryside, and it is likely that they generally came to be utilized as convenient drove roads when herds had to be moved from one district to another. To-day the boundaries can often be followed for miles along the ridges, sometimes the ditch or bank showing clearly, sometimes dwindling to little more than a pale line marked by upcast chalk and flints where rabbits have burrowed more freely in the soft soil of the ditch.

In many parts of Europe early literature describes how land boundaries were first drawn with a plough, a rite whose sacred meaning was often emphasized by special ceremonies. In this manner Romulus marked the bounds of Rome. After the first ritual demarcation, the line would often, of course, be reinforced with a trench or a fence. It is therefore of special significance to notice that the form of the British enclosure ditches with their narrow bottoms and gradually splaying sides is very reminiscent of a magnified furrow. When tracing these earthworks one can believe with some confidence that their line was first trodden by a Bronze Age ploughman who, not much less than 3000 years ago, urged on his oxen to cut in the turf the first furrow of ownership. We can feel a certain pride, moreover, in knowing that they are probably the most ancient boundaries of their kind surviving in western Europe.

For the proper handling of their flocks and herds the Deverel-Rimbury people banked or ditched rectangular kraals some quarter to two acres in extent. Such places would provide shelter for lambing and calving, and perhaps in the autumn the whole clan might assemble there to help with rounding up, slaughtering of surplus stock and the salting of meat for the winter larder.

For their more permanent homes many of them owned small steadings very like those built by the first Late Bronze Age settlers on Plumpton Plain (p. 106). Not many miles west of this older farm a Deverel-Rimbury family established itself on the summit of New Barn Down above Worthing. There a hollowed track led one along the down between the neat array of small fields, then, turning sharply across the ridge, entered a rectangular farmyard, protected on one side by a bank and ditch and on the others by a fence set on a low bank. Inside the enclosure rose the conical, thatched roofs of some half-dozen circular huts and barns, ranged round a small, open yard. It was a compact, well-planned little farm, where life could be ordered and secure, one of many scattered over the uplands of southern England.

A very different type of dwelling was chosen by a wealthy Late Bronze Age group in the north of England. Possibly the choice was not a free one, but forced upon them to escape some danger, otherwise it is difficult to understand why such people should want to live in a narrow, dark and excessively damp cave overlooking the little Heathery Burn, near Stanhope in County Durham. They occupied it long enough to break a great amount of crockery and to eat a great amount of beef, mutton and game, throwing the fragments and the bones cheerfully on the floor. Their equipment was astonishingly rich, including quantities of socketed axes, spears, swords, tools and ornaments and even a mould and tongs for the practice of bronze founding. An elegant shouldered bucket or *situla* (Fig. 12, bottom) and a golden armlet and ring must have been even more strangely out of place in these dank and wild surroundings. So many and excellent were their possessions that one cannot fail to wonder if the cave were the temporary home of an exiled chief and his followers. This idea gains colour from the fact that the group certainly included a bronze-smith and probably brought with them a four-wheeled horse-drawn cart, both of which are likely to have been the prerogatives of a man of rank. If one may be permitted a momentary flight of fancy, one can see the party fleeing after some defeat, possibly at the hands of the first Iron Age invaders (p. 123), the leader accompanied by his

FIG. 12. Bronze cauldron and bucket of the
Late Bronze Age (from Ireland).

retainers and his smith, forcing their way into these remote
regions, the once proud chariot dragged with difficulty over
rough, difficult country. And it is likely that their tenancy of
the cave had an even more violent conclusion. Why were so
many valuables abandoned on the floor, and why were the

bones of at least three human beings found among them? It seems that some catastrophe, probably a sudden spate in the ravine, must have caught them unawares, thus ending in tragedy a story which we believe began in misfortune.

Still farther to the north a little Late Bronze Age settlement was established at Jarlshof in the Shetlands, where a few stone-built houses sheltered among the dunes close by Sumburgh Head. The villagers lived simply but efficiently, making the best use of whatever was to hand in a country so cold and exposed as those islands. They kept herds of shorthorn cattle and two breeds of sheep, cultivated their fields, and also hunted seals and went fowling and fishing. Their solidly built houses were of a curious plan, perhaps first devised in the Mediterranean and then introduced here by the Megalithic folk. From a central courtyard with a hearth opened four little side-chambers contained in the thickness of the wall, while opposite the entrance was a large alcove which could serve as a cattle stall. One ingenious householder tethered his cattle to a stall-ring fashioned from a whale's vertebra, and appears also to have collected cowdung for his fields – the first recorded instance of the use of manure by a British farmer.

At first the community was as nearly self-sufficing as their Early Bronze Age predecessors at Skara Brae, fashioning their implements from bone and the local slate and quartz, and even carving domestic pots out of soft rocks. But towards the end of the Late Bronze Age an event occurred which must have caused great excitement among the simple villagers and served to link them with the outside world. A bronze-smith suddenly arrived in the hamlet, set up his workshop in one of the courtyards, and began to mould swords, knives, pins and other articles that must have impressed the locals as representing the height of luxury and scientific wonder. We can suppose that the smith, on the contrary, felt himself wretchedly benighted, and often cursed an unjust fate which had deprived him of his more comfortable livelihood farther south. For he may well have been one of the victims of the blacksmiths and their new metal, whose arrival in Britain threatened many of the bronze-founders with unemployment (p. 121).

If Late Bronze Age domestic arrangements show some improvement in the social amenities, the varied abundance of goods obtainable by the end of the period must have meant a much greater advance in the standard of living – and of killing. To consider the latter art first. The new offensive weapons, the sword, spear and axe already described, as they came to be produced more cheaply and in larger quantities, must have reached an ever-widening section of the population. At the same time defensive armament was reinforced. Warriors could now protect themselves with round shields, either wooden with a bronze boss over the handgrip, or all of bronze, the surface often enlivened by ring within ring of little *repoussé* knobs (Pl. 10A). Even horses might be armoured. One of the most magnificent objects surviving from this age is the great golden peytrel or horse's chest-piece that was found in a barrow at Mold in Flintshire (Pl. 10B). It is of fine sheet gold, mounted on bronze, and glitters with many rows of embossed designs that give a rich effect of light and shade.

Those invaders of south-east England who came from the Alpine lakes brought their own distinctive bronze types; their swords had parallel sides instead of bulging blades, and ended in a long, tapering, sinister-looking point, while their axes were a peculiar winged elaboration of the old flanged form (Fig. 10).

But improvement was not restricted to weapons of war:

men and women were also infinitely better equipped for their peaceful callings. Specialized tools were ready to the hand of the craftsman: socketed gouges and chisels for the carpenter, hammers, tracers, punches, tongs and miniature anvils for the bronze- and gold-smiths. To reap his increasing corn crops, the field worker could use a well-designed socketed sickle, while for the wealthy housewife cooking facilities were vastly improved by the introduction of sheet-bronze cauldrons (Fig. 12, top). In these great, fat, round-bellied vessels, fitted with ring handles for hanging them over the flames, food could be seethed and stewed in an appetizing manner hitherto impossible. Their design was copied by the Irish smiths from the Mediterranean, where such cauldrons are already often mentioned in Homeric verse. From Ireland they were imported as luxuries into Britain, a fact recalled by the tale in the Mabinogion that tells how a certain British king was the proud owner of one which had been brought over to him by an Irishman, 'a huge, reddish-yellow-haired man, coming up from the lake with a cauldron on his back'. Everwhere their possession was recognized as a certain mark of rank and wealth.

A second type of bronze vessel then in fashion, the *situla*, a high-shouldered bucket far more elegant and formal in taste than the portly cauldron, was an original Italian design that came to be widely imitated in western Europe (Fig. 12, bottom).

Other domestic crafts to advance their methods in the Late Bronze Age were spinning and weaving. For the first time there is evidence that spindles for twisting the yarn were weighted with round 'whorls' to increase their spin, while some form of upright loom was adopted in which the warp threads were held taut by cylindrical clay weights.

Improved weaving must have led to better clothes, and with them many ornaments were worn. Gold was still freely imported from Ireland. In contrast with this wealth of goods for the living, the dead were more poorly provided than at any other time in our prehistory, and there is an almost complete absence of new religious monuments of any kind. This need not mean that the Deverel-Rimbury people were stern rationalists, that a wave of agnosticism swept Britain in the Late Bronze Age; their religious tenets may even have been more spiritual and less superstitious than those held at other times, but certainly their beliefs did not impel them to great labours in the building of temples or tombs, or to great sacrifices for the enrichment of their dead. They had inherited from central Europe the custom of cremation burial in large cemeteries or 'urnfields'. The true central European urnfield had no grave-mounds, but in the west the old Battle-Axe warrior tradition was still sufficiently alive for low saucer-shaped barrows often to be raised over the cremations, or for the urns to be buried in the flanks of older tumuli. In Britain this persistence of the barrow idea was particularly strong in Wessex. No durable possessions went with the ashes into these cineraries, and the urns themselves, even at their most ornate, can show no more than plain lugs, flutings, or bands of clay corrugated with the impressions of the potter's finger-tips. Indeed, of all the dreary sights to be seen in our museums, none is more inevitably dreary than the contents of an aver-age large Deverel-Rimbury cemetery: row upon row of barrel-shaped or cylindrical urns, dark in paste, often lop-sided and ill-fired. Yet their very number, so wearying to the eye, has a special importance. It signifies the very great growth in population which better agriculture made possible by increasing food supplies, until by the end of the Late Bronze Age southern England was more thickly settled than ever before.

After 1300 years the British Bronze Age was reaching its

close. While in the north many of the old Urn Folk were still semi-nomadic pastoralists, the south was rich in settled hamlets and steadings surrounded by their arable fields and grazing grounds. Cheap bronze had made good tools and weapons available to many, and the merchants who supplied them grew in wealth and importance. There was better farming and craftsmanship, better clothes, more food and better cooking. Altogether a sufficiently prosperous land. Nor was the coming of the new age of iron to make any profound change in its structure. The bronze workers were naturally the hardest hit. These proud inheritors of a craft which in Britain had well over a millennium of tradition behind it had either to adapt themselves or succumb. In the Lowland Zone iron was gradually to displace bronze for the manufacture of tools and weapons, so that the founders were faced with the choice of learning to work iron, casting only the ornaments and fittings that continued to be made in the more beautiful old metal, or retreating to trade on a humbler scale in the Highland Zone, where bronze long held its own. We have already encountered one such impoverished merchant driven to seek his living at Jarlshof.

It was not that iron was at first greatly superior to bronze – indeed, it was little harder and in appearance far more uncouth – but that it was plentiful. Much of the bronze-smiths' power had depended on their knowledge and control of the sources of two raw materials: copper, which was far from common, and tin, which was even rarer. But with iron there was no need for such elaborate organization – ores could be found in abundance and in many places. Once its smelting was understood, once furnaces could be brought to a sufficient heat, iron could be produced far more cheaply and readily than bronze. Its adoption in Britain, therefore, really only intensified a social process already begun in the Late

Bronze Age – the putting of good tools and weapons within the reach of the many instead of the few.

Iron had been used by man very long before it was first brought to Britain. In Mesopotamia and Egypt it was occasionally used as early as 3000–2500 B.C. But it was the Hittites of Asia Minor who first began to work it on a large commercial scale, trading it freely among their neighbours in the eastern Mediterranean, and it was from them that the craft first reached Europe, where it became known to the Greeks by the end of the second millennium B.C. The warriors with iron swords whom we have seen driving out the Alpine Lake-dwellers after about 700 B.C. (p. 110) were sharers in the first widespread European iron-using civilization, that of Hallstatt, which originated in central Europe, but soon spread among the Celtic tribes of the west. At about this time the worsening of the climate which had flooded the lake villages began to have a serious effect on the farming communities of northern Europe. Threatened with famine, many were obliged to migrate southward, and it was mainly this cause, combined with a universal growth in population due to the development of agriculture, which sent further groups of Celts across the Channel, bearers of a late version of the Hallstatt culture. So it was that the first true British Iron Age began in southern England in the fifth century B.C.

CHAPTER V

The Early Iron Age

ALTHOUGH the use of iron was not general in Britain before the immigrations that began in the fifth century B.C., the vigorous Hallstatt civilization of central Europe, with its groups of restless swordsmen, did not fail to make itself felt at an earlier date. Already by the sixth century adventurers with knowledge of Hallstatt ways were percolating into these islands armed with swords that were usually made of bronze, yet followed the design of the iron weapon. Such pioneering groups exerted some influence on the Late Bronze population, and in particular we find the native bronze-smiths casting modified versions of their Hallstatt swords.

Some of them even arrived possessed of iron implements, and taught the smiths how to forge iron. One among them whom we may treat as representative of the rest was a warrior who seems to have sailed from western France to establish himself in south Wales on the fertile land of the Glamorgan Plain. Native hillsmen in the Black Mountains, envious of his property, organized a sally down to the Plain and looted his household. But as they were retreating triumphantly back towards their own fastnesses some alarm made them throw their booty into the mountain lake Llyn Fawr, where it was to lie for some two thousand five hundred years. The prize had been a rich one. It included two of the precious bronze cauldrons, which bobbed some little way across the surface of the lake before becoming water-logged and sinking. Then there was spearheads and axes of the ordinary Late Bronze type, but the chief had also owned a Hallstatt bronze razor and a sickle made of iron. The sickle had evidently been wrought by a native craftsman faithful to his traditional bronze patterns, however ill-suited to the new metal. Most remarkable of all was a great iron sword which, though native in some of its details, in form and size and in the curious winged shape which adorned its scabbard closely resembled the weapon carried by the Hallstatt swordsmen of the Continent (Fig. 10).

Settlers of this kind who used iron implements, and had the blacksmiths to forge them, acted as heralds of the true Iron Age which began in the fifth century B.C., when changes of climate and land shortage drove large numbers of fresh invaders to our shores. These came in several groups, landing all round our eastern and southern coasts, just as their precursors had done in the Late Bronze Age. The eastern seaboard received colonists from the Low Countries, among whom Hallstatt civilization was already much diluted, so far had they lived from its greatest centres. For this reason they were readily able to fuse with a British Bronze Age population with which they had much in common, and so build up a culture in which old traditions mingled with new. It was otherwise in Wessex, where Celts from northern France imposed a more advanced Hallstatt culture which took comparatively little from that of the old Deverel-Rimbury people.

If in much of the south of Britain this transition from the last Bronze to the first Iron Age was clear-cut, while in the east it was blurred, in neither did it very greatly change the habits of life developed during the previous centuries. The backbone of society continued to be the yeoman cultivator, who could turn warrior at will, and there is still little evidence for a disproportionately wealthy exploiting class.

This was the fifth century. While in Greece the poets, philosophers and sculptors of Periclean Athens were working for the enrichment of a beautiful and highly organized city state, Britain thus remained a simple agricultural land with scattered farmsteads and infrequent small villages. When looking down on the scatter of post-holes and pits marking the site of one of these modest Celtic farmsteads, it takes an effort to realize that without any very incredible chances its original owner might have found himself in classical Greece and watched the building of the Parthenon.

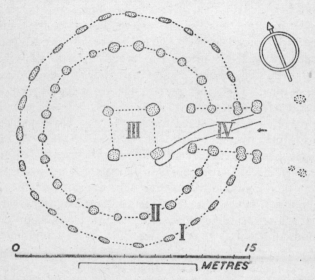

FIG. 13. Plan of Early Iron Age house, Little Woodbury, Wilts.

An Iron Age farm that well represents for us the kind of simple home achieved by the well-to-do members of the Wessex population stood at Little Woodbury, on the chalk downs overlooking the Avon valley a mile or so from the place where the spire of Salisbury cathedral was to rise some fifteen hundred years later. The farmer and his household (which may have included some of the live-stock) lived in a spacious round house (Fig. 13) standing in a circular fenced compound among the minor buildings and equipment of the farmyard. The busiest time to visit such a settlement would be the autumn. Then one could see the heads of corn carefully reaped with small sickles and hung on lines stretched between pairs of wooden posts. When the sun and wind had dried them, the grain would be winnowed in shallow depressions in the chalk, then divided into two parts, the larger for winter food, the smaller to be reserved as seed for the coming season. This seed corn, on which the hopes of the next season depended, had very special care, being stored in little square granaries, well ventilated and raised above the dampness of the ground. The other part of the crop, that which was intended for food, was dried in clay ovens to prevent germination before being poured for storage into deep, chalk-cut pits, roofed over and lined with basketry or skins. As grain-stores these pits had a short life, for after a few years they became infected with moulds and had to be abandoned: they were then commonly converted into rubbish-tips and filled with ashes, bones and all manner of domestic litter. During the course of some three centuries no fewer than three hundred and sixty such pits were sunk in the compound at Woodbury.

A household of this kind would be able to cultivate about 15 acres of arable, of which only one half or one third would be sown in any one year, while the downland grass offered good pasture for flocks of a small breed of sheep and a herd of shorthorn cattle. Below in the wooded valley pigs could find a living, and the farmer bring variety to his table by hunting red deer and other smaller game.

Farm equipment included the two-ox plough, perhaps now sometimes shod with iron, iron sickles, and querns for grinding flour by rubbing a smaller stone to and fro on a larger one.

Cloth was more than ever in demand, and the women must often have been seen sitting outside the house spinning yarn with the help of simple bone, pottery, or stone spindle whorls, or inside weaving at their looms with a line of triangular clay weights dangling from the warp threads. To separate and control these threads and to press down the woof they used well-made bone combs with long, decorated handles. Unhappily we shall probably never know the colour or designs of the fabrics cut from these Iron Age looms, nor

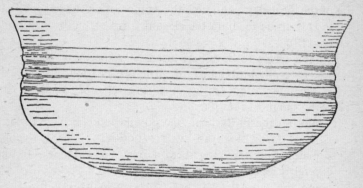

FIG. 14. Early Iron Age pottery bowl from Little Woodbury, Wilts.

much about the style of the clothes for wh ch they were intended.

The craft of potting, too, achieved a much higher standard than anything known in Britain before. Now for the first time there is the sharp distinction to which we have since grown accustomed between the 'best' service and the coarser kitchen ware. The fine crockery included shapely and thin-walled bowls (Fig. 14), some with simple geometric decoration cut on a glossy red surface. This attractive red colouring was obtained by dipping the pots in the iron oxide known as haematite to form a coating which was afterwards highly polished in imitation of bronze. One can imagine such bowls ranged on a shelf in an Iron Age farmhouse warmly lit by the fire and looking almost as attractive as a dresser full of old lustre.

The manufacture of such pieces demanded a special skill and knowledge which could hardly belong to the ordinary housewife. It was, in fact, carried on by experts, who seem to have traded their wares over quite wide areas. The simple cooking utensils, on the other hand, were made at home out of the local clays, although the women often strove to imitate in this crude medium the elegant form of the bronze *situla* (p. 119).

Iron seems to have been used only sparingly, or at least was carefully husbanded, for little is ever found in the early settlements: a few knives, pins, rings or other small objects being the most that remain.

Not all the Early Iron Age population can have lived in isolated farms such as Little Woodbury. Their dwellings sometimes clustered together on lower ground in groups that can fairly be called villages, a probable site of such a village being that at All Cannings Cross in Wiltshire. But these clusters were not nearly so common as we used to suppose when every grain-store was believed to represent a 'pit-dwelling', so that Little Woodbury would have been mistaken for a village of over three hundred houses! On this subject archaeologists have waged a stubborn battle. Clearly the imaginative appeal of the pit-dwelling is very great: there is something of the romantic savage in the picture of our ancestors passing their lives crouched in holes 10 feet below the ground. So great, indeed, is it that for long its supporters were blind to the evident truth that no human being could linger over a fire in such a pit and emerge alive. Cold reason, however, has been accepted in the end and banished the pit-dwellers from our history; instead it is recognized that these peasants had a practical means for storing the winter food necessary to support their increasing numbers.

As well as open villages there were strongholds on many hills, especially among the chalk downs of the south. The defences were slight enough at first – often a wooden palisade following the contours of the hilltop. Such places were probably intended primarily as temporary refuges for times of danger, even if farmers may sometimes have chosen to settle more permanently within their protective walls. Though unambitious in structure, these refuges already indicate a fair-sized social group united for its own security. And before long there were happenings which made such defence an imperative necessity.

While the Hallstatt Celts were quietly digging themselves into British soil, the expansion of the Celtic peoples had been causing widespread disturbance on the Continent. In the fourth century before Christ, Celts had crossed the Alps, conquered territory in Italy and sacked Rome; by the third they were pushing farther eastward, fighting the Macedonians, assailing Delphi and even crossing into Asia Minor, where they were to settle and become the 'foolish Galatians' of St Paul. Nor, as we have just hinted, did the West escape. In this same century their warrior bands crossed the Channel and caused panic among the population of Britain. With them into Britain they brought a culture that can no longer be called Hallstatt. Already when the first Hallstatt settlers were arriving in this country their kinsfolk in eastern France and south Germany were building up a new culture, that known as La Tène, which came to represent the height of early Celtic achievement. The Celts of these regions were helped to make this development from their old Hallstatt civilization by the stimulating contacts which they were receiving from the Mediterranean – particularly from the Etruscans of Italy and the prosperous Greek colonists of Marseilles. The Celts sent south such goods as backward peoples can usually supply to their more advanced neighbours, slaves and raw materials, above all metals, furs and amber from farther north. In exchange they imported a Mediterranean product for which they had developed a passionate desire: wine. With this wine came all the equipment for its proper enjoyment, fine bronze and pottery vessels for its carriage, storage, mixing and drinking. Chiefs might afford a whole table service of bronze wine vessels, many of which would be enriched with the stylized plant designs of classical convention. In this manner such patterns came before the eyes of the Celtic artist-craftsmen who were presently fired to adopt them as foundations for their own work. So that it has truly been said that 'La Tène art may largely have owed its existence to Celtic thirst.'

But no barbarian could merely imitate a Greek. The Celts soon transformed these borrowed conventions, with others that reached them from the Scythians of south-eastern Europe, into something inimitably their own; the orderly human spirit of classical taste fled before the free, flamboyant, visionary spirit which now inspired barbarian genius, to yield at last one of the most masterly abstract arts which Europe has known.

These good wines and lovely objects were for the gratification of a wealthy warrior aristocracy, for men such as those whose richly furnished graves are known by the Middle Rhine and in the Marne region of France. There they lay below covering mounds, buried in full pomp with lavishly ornamented sword and helmet, with their wine-flagons and their fighting chariots. It seems that it was about 250 B.C.

that numbers of such warriors began, as we have seen, to cross to Britain, sailing probably from the mouth of the Seine, and introduce for the first time the La Tène culture which was to bear its final and most mature fruits in these islands.

The consternation which their coming provoked among the British peasants was not without practical results. The inhabitants began hastily to throw up defence works; farmers, such as the owners of Woodbury dug ditches round their homesteads and strengthened their fences, while hilltops were crowned with quite formidable forts, sometimes replacing the older palisaded strongholds (p.129). Hardly less familiar landmarks than the long and round barrows are these 'camps' which crown so many of our hills, their defences following the natural contours. Probably many of the earliest were put up at this time in the third century before Christ against the inroads of La Tène warriors from northern France. Their building was a formidable effort, even more formidable than their present appearance suggests. To-day, though impressive in scale, they look simple enough (Pl. 15): a single turf-covered bank sloping gradually into a mild, grassy ditch: from a distance no more than a tiny nick in the profile of the hill. But this form is the outcome of collapse and decay. Picture them as they were when new-built and ready for defence. The attacker was first confronted with a steep-sided ditch cut deep into the chalk; beyond lay a narrow strip of level ground under direct fire from the ramparts, which presented an almost sheer wall of timbers or coursed turf or stone secured by stout uprights. Against the back of this revetment the chalk bank was piled, its top making a protected rampart wall for the defenders. At the weakest point in the circuit, the entrance, the rampart might swing inwards so that the wooden gates stood inset at the end of a funnel-like entry which could be raked by cross-fire.

One can imagine the scene so well – the dead white of the newly dug chalk, the raw feel and smell of the fresh timber, the wood-chippings scattered on the trampled ground.

So sudden and short were the onsets of danger that these early forts were often abandoned unfinished, and few were occupied for long. The determined and organized resistance to aggression which they represent discouraged the La Tène raiders and prevented them from settling in any force on the southern chalk. Groups of them did settle here and there, certainly in Sussex round the great fort of Cissbury near Worthing, and in places in Wessex and east Kent, and these brought perceptible changes into the old Hallstatt traditions, but no wholly La Tène type of society was established. Other groups seem to have penetrated beyond the Thames – into East Anglia, for example – establishing their power over the Hallstatt peasantry. Here must be the origin of the royal line of the Iceni which was to end bloodily and heroically in the great queen Boudicca.

In Scotland a rather more substantial colonization took place when, in the third century B.C., or later, invaders overcame a native population still mainly living in a belated Bronze Age. They soon spread right across the middle of the country, between its eastern and south-western coasts. They it was who built the so-called vitrified forts of Scotland, such as those well known at Castle Law near Abernethy and Finavon in Angus. It has recently been shown by practical experiment that this vitrification or fusing of the rock of which they are built was not deliberate. The forts were in fact originally built by the curious method which Caesar found still in use among the Gauls: stone facings were bonded together with vertical and horizontal timbers, and more wood went into the rubble core. When such a building was set on fire, accidentally or by an enemy, the timbers burnt away, and their sockets made such efficient flues that enough heat was generated to melt and fuse the stones. The final but unintentional product was a vitrified fort.

But it was in eastern Yorkshire and Lincolnshire that the newcomers established their most characteristic colonies. There La Tène chiefs ruled their followers and the native population with an absolutism that allowed them to maintain more of their Continental habits and standards. The tribe to settle in east Yorkshire was that of the Parisi, who still held that territory when Ptolemy was writing four centuries later. Coming as they did from northern France, we can safely recognize them as an offshoot of the people whose name has been so conspicuously preserved in that of the French capital. It is an amusing thought that such an historical link should exist between the Parisian and the Yorkshire tyke.

In this north-eastern region, more than any other, society fell into a highly aristocratic pattern, recalling that of the Early Bronze Age. Wealth and power were concentrated in the hands of a small minority who formed a world of relative luxury. In that world it seems that women could occupy a high and honourable place.

Much thought was given to personal appearance. The men wore cloaks or plaids fastened at the shoulder with safety-pin brooches sometimes studded with coral, and hung wrists and ankles with bronze or jet bangles. With wealth and leisure the amiable vice of vanity could be cultivated, and we find a La Tène lady sophisticated enough to employ polished metal hand-mirrors in making her toilet.

The chiefs' weapons were of the finest. They carried

133

iron-bladed daggers, the bronze hilt often in the form of a manikin with splayed arms and legs, and short iron swords sheathed in bronze scabbards that might be richly chased with La Tène designs. For defence they had oval wooden shields with ornamental mountings in bronze, and perhaps occasionally helmets.

These heroes no longer had to go into battle on foot, but drove in the two-wheeled chariots which the Celts had adopted from the Etruscans of Italy. The chariots were wooden, and had spoked iron-tyred wheels standing rather less than three feet high. By Caesar's time at least, they opened forwards to allow the warrior to dart recklessly down the shaft-pole between the pair of horses when he wished better to reach an adversary or cast a javelin. From snaffle-bits of surprisingly modern design (Pl. 16B) the reins passed through decorated bronze terret rings into the hands of the charioteer, whose duty it was to manoeuvre the vehicle for his warrior master.

When admiring the beauty of La Tène weapons and trappings, it is well to remember that the resplendent aristocrats under whose patronage they were made probably passed their everyday lives in squalor. Their houses were of the simplest – round huts lacking in domestic amenities. It was in part this combination of lavish personal display with graceless living that the Greeks and Romans despised in their barbarian neighbours.

In an aristocratic society of this type it is not surprising to find a return to elaborate and expensive funerary rites. The dead were laid in pits below small, round barrows, fully clad and decked with ornaments, and, just as in France, they might be accompanied by their war chariots, sometimes complete, more often dismantled. It was only a very great man who could hope to be furnished with horses; normally they were too valuable for sacrifice, and their harness alone went into the grave. Very frequently large joints of pork or whole pigs were buried, and even the humbler graves were supplied with a leg standing in an earthenware jar. This custom probably implies more than a strong preference for

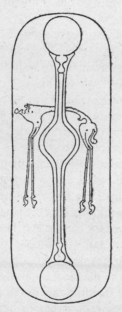

FIG. 15. The Witham shield :
outline-diagram showing ornamental boar-figure.

pork; as game highly prized by a hunting aristocracy, the boar had a special prestige – a religious significance even greater than that now enjoyed in this country by the fox. Accordingly we find pigs portrayed by Celtic artists in a manner suggesting special honours, the most remarkable examples being the strange attenuated creature that straddles the Witham shield (Fig. 15) and the spirited little bronze beast from Hounslow (Pl. 11A) that probably once crested some warrior's helmet.

The greatest contribution to history made by this north-eastern La Tène colony was in the work of its artists. During the centuries which followed its foundation they more than any of their contemporaries were responsible for the growth of a British school of decorative art which is one of the outstanding episodes in the story of our civilization.

Their achievement has mainly to be judged from the metalwork which has survived where a mass of lovely but perishable things must have disappeared. But it is enough to show that these artists happily combined the surest sense of plastic form with an equal mastery of decorative design in the flat. Their plastic skill is admirably shown in the horse-bits already mentioned (Pl. 16B): one feels that aesthetically the craftsman who conceived them could do no wrong. A snaffle-bit like this is wholly practical, yet so perfect are the proportions, the curves and the mouldings that the whole is a certain work of art. The same mastery can be still better appreciated by studying Pl. 12, the detail of a bronze sacrificial dish from Celtic Ireland. In surface decoration the earliest style is still based on renderings of classical plant forms, but these were conceived in a Celtic freedom that developed towards a pure geometric style, a style of dynamic pattern, the poise of which stiffened into a duller and more formal symmetry only when touched by the influence of Rome.

One of the loveliest individual masterpieces of the early designers is the sword dredged from the river Witham (Pl. 9). The bronze scabbard mount curls up and over in curves as free and unpredictable as a sea-wave. Another most dramatic piece designed a little later is the Torrs champfrein or horse's head-armour, an object which both in its form and in the decoration of its surface is extraordinarily striking and forceful. Though much later in date, the fine bronze mirrors from Birdlip and Desborough (Fig. 19) are evidently part of the same flow of genius, as is also that great national treasure the Battersea shield (Pl. 13), but we shall find that here fresh currents are augmenting the stream (p. 156). This later phase, which led to the final one when British La Tène art was first debased and then suppressed by the alien traditions of Rome, belongs more properly to the next chapter.

Meanwhile, and long before our Celtic art had reached the advanced stage to which we have now followed it, another region of Britain was receiving La Tène immigrants. The motives which took them from west France to south-western England seem to have been rather different from those operating elsewhere. Here in the south-west it was not only to plunder and seize land that they came; they were pursuing trade, even if it was at the sword's point. The tin of west Cornwall had been a major factor in the Bronze Age economics of western Europe, and now once more this peninsula was invaded by warrior traders who saw that its control would bring them wealth. Here we get the first glimpse of recorded British geography. The daring Greek explorer Pytheas visited Cornwall in about 325 B.C., and to him is ascribed the famous account of how its people mined and smelted the tin and brought it across in waggons at low tide to the island of Ictis, whence continental merchants took it by ship to the west French coast, and so overland to the mouth of the Rhône and the markets of Mediterranean civilization. Unless the coastline has changed, Ictis is most likely to be St Michael's Mount, and the trade evidently supported a large mining population in the tin-bearing regions round about and kept them in touch with the Continent.

Conquest and exploitation here meant a rich prize for the

La Tène adventurers, and since the earlier inhabitants were not warlike, and probably but little advanced beyond the material level of the Late Bronze Age, the prize may have been easily won. But to secure their hold the invading leaders needed fortified strongholds. We have already seen how the descendants of the Hallstatt people in Wessex and elsewhere built hill-forts against the La Tène invaders of the third century B.C. The same thing may have been tried here and there against our south-western invaders, but the strongholds which they built for their own security, though standing likewise on hill or upland sites, are forts of a distinctive type, with a strictly circular ground-plan. In west Cornwall such stone-walled ringforts as Chun Castle are prominent features of the landscape, and often stand above a contemporary hamlet, much as a medieval baron's castle at once protects and overawes its village.

The hamlets here were also distinctive. A typical one, dominated by the fort of Castle-an-Dinas, was that of Chysauster, south-west of St Ives, which lasted from late in this period into Roman times. It had at least eight houses, built on the courtyard plan (p. 117), flanking a cobbled street: these were surrounded by garden plots and small arable fields, and the inhabitants were not only cultivators, but also miners and smelters of tin. Both fort and village dwellers made and used the subterranean galleries which the Cornish know as fogous. These were apparently hiding-places against attack, and, whatever their origin, they go with the forts to show that violence and warfare now loomed large in all men's lives.

Farther east, in Cornwall, there were fewer fogous, but more ringforts, such as Castle Dore near Fowey, within which the inhabitants dwelt in timber-built round huts. Farther east again, this south-western culture came closer

138

to the main stream of British civilization, and fort-building drew more on the older contour-plan tradition described above (p. 131), issuing presently in imposing new developments.

By the beginning of the first century B.C. the increasingly warlike character of Celtic civilization was in this corner of Britain enhanced by the rise of a new weapon, the sling. With this simple loop of leather, a man could hurl a smooth pebble or a baked clay bullet with great force at comparatively long range, to smite his enemy as David smote Goliath, and organized companies of slingers could play as deadly a part in battle as riflemen in more modern warfare. The art of the sling came probably along the tin route from the western Mediterranean, where for example Balearic slingers were so famous, and the development of the art of fortification to suit it was apparently begun by the Veneti, the coastal people of Brittany who plied most of the cross-Channel trade with south-western Britain. The main feature was to multiply the number of your lines of defence, to set the greatest possible distance between yourself inside them and the attacking enemy outside. This multiplication of ramparts was, it seems, first applied to the 'cliff castles' with which these people fortified the promontories of their rocky coast, and the application was perhaps first generally made when all ancient France or Gaul was invaded by the wild Cimbric and Teutonic tribes from northern Europe, just before 100 B.C. Similar cliff castles, evidently the work of these same Veneti or their British associates, stand thick along the coasts of Cornwall, and the principle of multiple ramparts, suited to sling warfare, was also extended inland, for ring-forts and soon also for hill-top fortresses of larger size, contour-planned in the older native tradition.

The result was a gradual spread of hill-fortification on a

great scale, from the south-west northward and eastward, wherever aggression or colonization by the south-westerners, or imitation of them by other tribes, carried the new sling warfare. Neither at first made much headway in Wessex; the famous Maiden Castle near Dorchester, originally a moderate-sized fort of the older native type, was early in this phase enlarged, but with only a single ditch and rampart, and by the Wessex natives, not the south-western aggressors.

It was from Cornwall and Devon coastwise along the Bristol Channel that the new art of war spread mainly. Some groups of trading colonists were probably going this way already, for example to Bredon Hill fort, on the edge of the Cotswolds, but more followed and on both sides of the Severn. The iron of the Forest of Dean was probably one of their major objectives, and there was coastal settlement farther west in Wales, while others began to move northward into the country of the Marches. Presently all this quarter of Britain was by warfare, trade, and migration linked together in a loose cultural unity, of which the forts serve as an abiding sign.

But by far the most remarkable centres of La Tène culture which are known in this region are protected not by fortification, but by water – the Somerset lake-villages of Meare and Glastonbury. These were settled later than the first invasions into Cornwall, and it may well be that further immigrants from Brittany, to be noticed later (p. 155), had a share in their foundation, or at least development; but their excavation has given us an exceptionally full picture of the life of the period. The Glastonbury village, lying about a mile north of the modern town, is the better known. It was excellently placed for trade, being connected by the Mendips with the main upland system of British trackways, and within coastwise reach of the Cornish tin exporters, as well as in direct touch southward with the shores of the Channel. For the security which the stormy times demanded, the founders of the village chose a piece of marshy ground that probably became completely flooded in winter and spring. Well equipped with iron billhooks, they hacked down the growth of alder and willow which cumbered the site, and then, with immense labour, went on to build up an artificial island on the ground they had cleared. Its main bulk was a bed of horizontal logs, close-packed and sometimes as much as 4 feet in thickness, but it was made yet more substantial with clay, stones, brushwood, and bracken, much of which had to be carted from a distance. To prevent it from spreading, they bounded their island with a stout palisade of vertical timbers driven well down into the marsh, the tops projecting to form a strong fence.

At the height of its prosperity this man-made island exceeded 10,000 square yards in extent, and on it stood some sixty round huts with wattled sides, trodden clay floors, and roofs thatched with reeds. Each house had a stone or clay hearth in the centre of the floor, and some had paved doorsteps, while cobbled alley-ways led between them. The village would first appear to the visitor as a huddle of thatched roofs rising among the thickets of alders and willows; carts are bringing produce from the higher ground where the villagers keep their beasts and cultivate corn and vegetables, while dug-out canoes moored at a landing-stage are ready for fowling expeditions among the many waterways, or for longer trading excursions. Inside its protecting wall, the village itself is full of life and activity – a compact stronghold of humanity isolated among the swamps. Duck and coot can be heard calling and splashing among reeds where herons and cranes stand motionless; occasionally a bittern sounds its uncanny, booming call; and there, top-heavy, comical, and grotesquely beautiful, a family of pelicans is sailing down the open waterway. The villagers naturally avail themselves of all this wild life over their fence to add seasonable variety to their meals: they enjoy wildfowl of many kinds, especially duck, and also such freshwater fish as perch, roach, and trout.

Indeed, in all ways their industry and enterprise gave them a high standard of life. Carpenters were highly skilled and ambitious. Their accomplishments ranged from the heavy work of constructing platforms and houses, and of hollowing canoes, through cart-building and beautiful wheelwright's work, to such delicate operations as the lathe-turning of wooden vessels (Fig. 16) and the carving of ladles and graceful handles for iron implements. This iron equipment was itself varied and efficient. Blacksmiths' designs have changed little through the centuries, and Glastonbury sickles and bill-hooks (Fig. 16) hardly differ from those used to trim our own hedges and ditches, while neat little saws, as well as chisels and gouges, were forged for the carpenters. Bronze still had many uses. A sheet-bronze bowl ornamented with large hollow rivet-heads is one of the prides of Glastonbury town, where somewhat tinny reproductions can be bought as souvenirs – an honour which would surely have surprised and delighted its one-time owners. Among more domestic crafts, weaving was much practised; the same long-handled combs (Fig. 16) were popular as those used by the women of the earlier Iron Age, but an improvement of method is shown by, the trim little bone bobbins which carried the yarn in wooden shuttles. Another important labour-saving device – invented long since in the East – was the rotary quern for grinding corn. For nearly two thousand years, ever since the introduction of cereals for food in Neolithic times, house-wives had been content to make their flour by pushing one

142

stone to and fro over another. Now they had only to turn a handle to revolve an upper stone pivoted in the neither one.

The Glastonbury people – perhaps it was again the women – were excellent potters. Their products are famous among

FIG. 16. The Glastonbury Lake Village: weaving comb, handle, dicebox, billhook and wooden tub.

all our prehistoric wares for the rich La Tène decoration which was engraved on smoothly-rounded bowls or fat, comfortable-looking pots rather like Chinese ginger-jars. The incised patterns are often both ingenious and pleasing, though a certain stiffness is introduced by the frequent use of compasses in laying out the designs – a matter to which we shall return below (p. 156). When the wheel principle was in use not only for vehicles and for querns, but even for turning wooden vessels, it is surprising to find that the fast-turning potter's wheel was apparently still unknown. The Glastonbury villagers have perhaps been made to sound excessively industrious; but they were not above gambling, with dice to throw from carefully carved boxes (Fig. 16). Probably the strongest impression one gets from the village is that the art

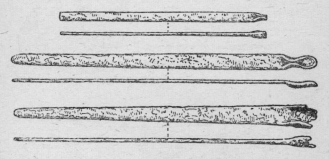

FIG. 17. Iron currency-bars of the Iron Age.

which had formerly been enjoyed only by the Celtic aristocracy had here spread, simplified in form but still admirable in taste, to the common people and their everyday works and surroundings.

Their general standard of culture was perhaps unusually high, for they were evidently much of a trading community, importing Cornish tin, lead from Mendip, Dorset shale, glass beads and amber from the Continent, and, probably mainly from the Forest of Dean, much iron, which went not only to make tools, weapons, and useful appliances of many kinds, but to furnish the medium of commerce itself – that is, a currency. This took the form of long, flat iron bars (Fig. 17), pinched up at one end, perhaps derived from the rough-outs for sword-blades, but standardized in weight. They must have been very cumbersome to handle, but are found here and over a wide area in the south-west of Britain, testifying further to its unity of culture, and to its outside connexions also, since they extend into Wessex, the Thames valley, and the Midlands. The way across the Midland forests was marked by the belt of Jurassic rock-subsoil which makes a corridor of open country from the Cotswolds over into Lincolnshire, and there is an important ring-fort on this line at Hunsbury near Northampton, where the local ironstone was worked and a variety of remains shows a culture very like that of the Somerset villages, though it began earlier and did not survive as late. This way went the main connexions with the north, where the Parisian and other La Tène peoples were still flourishing, their more distant venturers now even reaching the north of Ireland.

And the other way went the connexions with the Continent across the western end of the Channel, where the sailing-galleys of the Veneti plied between Britain and Brittany. Though an iron anchor and its chain are known from a fort near Poole Harbour, actual remains of those galleys have never yet been found. But their description has come down to us, written by the man who brought their power to an end. That man was Julius Caesar, the Roman conqueror of Gaul, who in 56 B.C. met the defiance of the tribes of Brittany in a great sea battle off their coast, and utterly destroyed their assembled fleet. The next year he addressed himself to the invasion of Britain.

CHAPTER VI

Britain and the Romans

IT may seem strange to the English reader, for whom going abroad has usually meant Dover to Calais, that the broad Atlantic end of the Channel should ever have served for a main crossing between his island and the Continent. But this Brittany crossing was, of course, part of the ancient Atlantic sea-route, and it connected the metal-bearing west with the easiest ancient way to the markets of the Mediterranean, past the mouth of the Loire and across south-west France. On the other hand, the Straits of Dover, until near the end of prehistoric times, lay between regions not particularly wealthy or important in themselves, and not particularly connected with the more distant centres of European civilization. Only when occasional major folk-movements broke into the sequestered corner of France did they bear any very distinguished traffic. But as the Iron Age wore on, major folk-movements became more frequent and more formidable; in particular, while the Mediterranean civilization that became the Roman Empire was spreading from the south, the Germanic peoples had begun to press down from the north. Their climate had been getting colder and wetter, and, with better farming and the introduction of iron, their population bigger and their armament stronger. One of their outlets was across the Rhine in this direction.

As early as Hallstatt times, their pressure this way had been one of the causes of Celtic migration to Britain, and by the time the Cimbric and Teutonic tribes mentioned in the last chapter broke through into Gaul and beyond, there had been much Germanic infiltration among the Celts of the

Low Countries, and a mixed Celtic population of similar Germanic tinge had succeeded to the older La Tène culture of the Marne (p. 130). These peoples were called Belgae, and at the beginning of the first century B.C. they had spread west to cover most of the country between the lower Rhine and the lower Seine with their own latter-day version of La Tène civilization. The lands directly across the Straits from Britain were thus drawn into that civilization much more fully than before, and their population increased. At the same time German aggression moved south and grew stronger. Presently the Celtic tribe of the Helvetii, pressed between the upper Rhine and the Swiss Alps, could bear it no longer, and determined to migrate in a body towards the west. Their departure would have left a great breach for German entry into Gaul; and it is at this point, in 58 B.C., that Julius Caesar arrives upon the scene.

The growing power of the Romans had some time before annexed what is now the south of France, and Caesar's object now was not only to keep the Germans out, but to annex the whole country for Rome. Ultimately, he succeeded. We have already seen how in the course of his famous campaigns he conquered the Veneti of Brittany. But the Belgae in the northeast had given him much hard fighting in the previous year, and he had not been at this long before he found that they were being helped from Britain, where, just across the Straits of Dover, they had kinsmen of their own, who had migrated thither less than a generation before. The Belgae, in fact, had overflowed into south-eastern Britain, and had made the lands they had settled provinces of Belgic culture.

Remains of this Belgic culture have often been discovered. The Belgae, like the Germans, cremated their dead, and they buried the ashes in shapely urns, usually pear-shaped and often with a pedestal foot, which are sometimes found grouped in cemeteries or urnfields. The best known are in Kent, where they settled first: Swarling, near Canterbury, and Aylesford on the Medway. In most graves the urn was accompanied by other pots, no doubt to hold funeral offerings of food and drink, and sometimes by bronze or even silver brooches, shaped like a large and ornate safety-pin. At Aylesford there were also bronze vessels – a pan and wine-jug – from Italy, and a great wooden bucket bound and handled in bronze, with two unearthly-faced human heads frowning above the rim, and designs beaten out on the upper band, including strange, leafy-tailed horse-monsters. Here we have a fresh instalment of La Tène art from Gaul; yet it is not for such isolated treasures that the Belgae are most notable, but rather for their more efficient and better-equipped mastery of the arts of everyday life.

They made pottery on the true potter's wheel; their iron-work, of which there will be more to say presently, was superlative, as was their woodwork also, and in addition to warlike and domestic gear they made a new heavy type of plough, mounted on wheels in front and armed with a big coulter to cut the sod and mould-boards to turn it. Whereas the old, light, two-ox plough could only scratch a superficial furrow even in easy soils, this new plough enabled them to till comparatively heavy ground, which they could first clear of timber with their iron axes; and so there began something of a revolution in British agriculture and land settlement. Thus, while the scattered farmsteads in which they mainly lived were still primitive as dwellings – simple round or oval huts for the most part – their produce nourished a thriving population. And Belgic fighting strength carried still farther the dominance of warfare over Iron Age life. They fought on foot, on horseback, and from chariots, and though they had not developed the same art of multiple fortification as the western peoples, they could make formidable hill-forts enough, on woodland sites for choice, with defences often relying especially on a steep and wide main ditch. And in twenty years from their first coming they had spread from Kent to the Thames, and from the Thames deep into northern Hertfordshire.

Caesar's judgement of the situation was that the security of a conquered Gaul demanded a conquered Britain. Accordingly, in August 55 B.C. he made a start by crossing from Boulogne with some 10,000 men, to explore, and, if all went well, to force obedience at least on the Belgae of eastern Kent. But all did not go well: his fleet was damaged by a stormy high tide on the beach near Deal, and the local tribes with their chariots and horsemen gave his army some very sharp encounters. He therefore got the expedition back to Gaul as soon as he could, and prepared for a larger one next year. Elaborate preparations were made, and about midsummer he crossed again, with a much larger force; he struck inland at once, and stormed the Belgic hill-fort of Bigbury near Canterbury – but only to learn that his fleet had once more been damaged by a storm. While it was being repaired, the Kentish tribes allied themselves with the leading Belgic chieftain beyond the Thames in Hertfordshire. This was Cassivellaunus, an aggressive leader, against whom Caesar's assistance had already been sought by one of the non-Belgic tribes, the Trinovantes, who lived in Essex. Cassivellaunus knew he could not withstand the Roman legions in a pitched battle, but by skilful mobile warfare he harassed their advance over Kent, and again after they had crossed the Thames and reached the Trinovantes. At last Caesar found and stormed his hill-fort capital at Wheathampstead; but even then the Romans had to beat off a fresh onslaught by his Kentish allies on their naval base. By early autumn he came to terms;

but though Caesar imposed on him an annual tribute, and a promise to leave the Trinovantes alone, the great Roman general retired to Gaul aware that Britain had really not been conquered at all. The fame of Cassivellaunus' resistance lived on ever afterwards in British story, but Caesar soon found that to conquer Gaul itself he needed several more years of bitter fighting, while he had only marked down Britain for conquest in the future.

Caesar's account of his invasions and of Britain generally, given us in his famous *Commentaries*, is the earliest surviving piece of written history concerned with our island. But he did not get beyond one corner of it, and by setting what he has told us against a background of modern knowledge, we can fill out his picture in many ways. It is clear that through the Belgic colonization, the corner which he visited had for the first time become the most powerful and most civilized, as civilization then went. It is clear also that the non-Belgic inhabitants hated and feared the Belgae, and opposed their expansion. The Trinovantes were even glad to take sides with Caesar against Cassivellaunus, and between Wheathampstead, their enemy's capital fortress, and St Albans, where his successors presently settled, a great Belgic boundary ditch may still be seen, along the valley known as Beech Bottom. To dig this 100 feet wide and over 30 feet deep as they did, the intruders must indeed have been uneasy at first in their adopted land. The Wheathampstead fortress ditch is even bigger, and the tale of hostility between the Belgae and their neighbours is not confined to Hertfordshire.

In Kent their southern flank ran along the wooded fringes of the Weald, and here the inhabitants protected themselves against them by building large hill-forts like Oldbury Camp near Ightham. These inhabitants were largely an offshoot of the earlier La Tène immigrants into Sussex, whose expansion over the Wealden forest was no doubt connected with its important deposits of iron ore. There is evidence that the Kentish Belgae also worked Wealden iron, while, as we shall see, their fellows north of the Thames ultimately reached the ironstone region of Northants and Oxfordshire. From the ores thus won, reduced in clay-built furnaces, the Belgic smiths forged their weapons of war, their chariot- and harness-fittings, their implements of forestry and farming, and the furnishings of their chieftains' hearths. These last were superb iron firedogs rising at either end to the likeness of a knob-horned ox-head, which display a true artist's feeling for fitness of design in wrought metal (Pl. 16A). But the westerners' iron bar-currency, which they met with in the Thames valley and beyond, they did not make, for they brought with them from Gaul what was perhaps the most momentous of all the inventions adopted by La Tène from Mediterranean civilization – coinage.

Celtic coinage on the Continent was imitated from Greek, and in central Gaul was first minted in the second century B.C. Early in the next century gold coins of the Belgic Gauls began to circulate in south-east Britain, first those of the Bellovaci (from the district where Beauvais still preserves their tribal name), and then, starting in Kent, where the earliest Belgic colonists settled, those of the Atrebates (from the district of Arras). Such Gaulish types may sometimes have been actually minted over here, and the first distinguishably British coins took their type from an Atrebatic model. The designs of both faces look quite extraordinarily meaningless, until one sees them and their Gaulish models side by side with the Greek type from which they were ultimately derived (Fig. 18). This was the standard gold coin of the famous King Philip of Macedonia (the father of Alexander the Great), and it has on one side the head of the god

151

Apollo wearing a laurel wreath, and on the other a driven chariot with two horses. The successive Celtic imitators, to whom the whole idea was strange, reduced both designs in time to uncouth patterns, the head perishing in a maze of blobs crossed by a sort of herring-bone version of the wreath, and the chariot and pair broken up into another maze of blobs, in which one can just see the dismembered skeleton of what once was a horse. But gradually after that the head design was worked out in Britain into a regular cross-pattern,

Fig. 18. Ancient British coins and (on extreme left)
one of their Greek models.

based on the old wreath. And the never quite forgotten horse on the other side was suddenly created afresh, prancing in a weird but animated life. The famous White Horse of Uffington (Pl. 15) is probably a gigantic rendering of the same new form of strange, half-supernatural creature, cut in the chalk of the Berkshire Downs by a people who boasted him as a tribal or religious emblem. And that brings us back to our main story. For this people were for the most part fresh Belgic settlers from Gaul, who, when Caesar was at last victorious there, would not submit to Roman rule, but took refuge in Britain instead.

Caesar in both his expeditions had used the services of the king of the Atrebates, whose name was Comm or Commius. He was a person of some standing not only in Gaul, but in Britain, where we have seen his people's coinage circulating in Kent. Later he turned against Caesar, and when the Gaulish resistance was broken he fled to Britain, with shiploads of followers. This was about 50 B.C., and in due course coins inscribed with the name of Commius are found in Britain; not indeed in Kent, where one would not expect him after his association with the hated Roman, but farther west. There, between the west Sussex coast and the middle Thames, they follow after those with the new type of horse from Gaul just mentioned, and also after a local version of the coinage of his own tribe, the Atrebates. It looks as if Atrebatic and other refugees from Gaul settled in these regions in various tribal groups – the new horse on the coins was perhaps contributed by Remi from the district of Reims – which Commius eventually made into a single kingdom.

Like their relatives in the south-east, these people were not only stout warriors: they introduced improved farming and other peaceful arts, and their coins replaced the old native currency of iron bars. Their pottery was made on the wheel, and it is by this that the remains of their settlements are most easily recognized. But, unlike the south-eastern Belgae, they came as survivors of a culture broken by the conquest of their homes, and thus it is natural to find its potters' art reduced among them to a much-diminished range, the commonest type of vessel being a simple bowl or jar with a plain beading for a rim. Such bowls were also used as urns for burying the ashes of their cremated dead.

Commius seems to have died about 20 B.C., and by then the new Belgic lands probably stretched into Wessex as far west as the river Test, which has its mouth in Southampton

153

Water. They included the Isle of Wight, but the chief harbour was by Chichester, where the first landings had probably been, thirty years before. Here there is a regular series of defensive ditches suggesting the Belgic manner (p. 150), and it must have been the Belgae who brought the native occupation to a sudden end at the old hill-fort of the Trundle, overlooking Goodwood racecourse on the downs above. Then farther inland they had wrecked the native fort on St Catharine's Hill above Winchester by fire, and taken for their own the native settlements on the neighbouring downs, as they did the virgin site of Winchester itself. Apart from a few fortified capitals, the Belgæ needed hill-strongholds themselves only in the frontier lands where they fought continually with the natives to extend their territory.

The natives, for their part, built or renewed hill-forts of their own against them. In Wessex the strong forts characteristic of this time begin just west of the line where the circulation of the Belgic coins described above leaves off, the line of the river Test, whose steep-sided, marsh-bottomed valley cuts a frontier like a curving trough across the chalk downs of Hampshire. Their defences are variously planned, but most of them have multiple ramparts and ditches, such as we have already seen introduced into the south-west by the Veneti from Brittany, and some have a more or less circular plan like the south-western ring-forts. Where such works are renewals of abandoned earlier forts, they may form a strong citadel inside the old rampart, as at Bury Hill and Danebury near Andover, or else, as at Yarnbury Castle north-west of Salisbury, an enlarged circuit surrounding it. The farther one goes west, the longer the inhabitants were able to withstand Belgic encroachment, and the more imposing are the forts. The grandest of all is the renowned Maiden Castle in Dorset, where the earlier fort, already enlarged

(p. 140), was now transformed (Pl. 14): the new multiple works brought its size to close on 100 acres, and the inner rampart, towering at least 50 feet above the bottom of its fronting ditch, was massively built in chalk and earth and clay and limestone masonry, the limestone laboriously brought from outcrops over two miles away. The entrance defences were as complex as they were formidable, and the 45 acres of the space within made now no mere occasional camp of refuge, but a permanently inhabited township, the capital of the nameless chief whose will raised this stupendous fortress.

His domain was 70 miles westward from the first footholds of the Belgae on the Chichester coast, and they did not reach and conquer it for some seventy years. The military architecture which served to hinder them so long was, in fact, first brought to central Dorset by more western folk from Gaul, probably the fighting remnant of the Breton Veneti themselves, when Caesar had broken their power across the Channel in 56 B.C. Like their relations earlier in Cornwall and along the Severn Sea, they were warrior adventurers, and with their swords and spears and deadly sling-stones they forced themselves by conquest upon the natives, and secured their hold in these great forts, just as the Norman conquerors of later England did in their castles. Under their rule, the farming life of the countryside went on virtually unaltered, and the round houses and granary store-pits of the traditional sort were still made much as before. But they did introduce a new kind of pottery to the lingering Hallstatt tradition, bowls and jars with a bead-rim rather like the Belgic, but of simpler form, and made without the potter's wheel, often with loop handles sunk in the body on either side.

These territories shared in the general south-western circuit of trade and metal-working, and they used the iron bar-currency, but later took to coinage modelled on the Belgic. By then the neighbouring Dobuni, as the people of the Cotswolds and the lower Severn were called, had begun to issue coins bearing the names of kings, with designs based on Belgic models, and the Iceni of the eastern counties, and the Brigantes centred in western Yorkshire, had done the same. The coins of the Dorset people were uninscribed, but we know that their tribal name was the Durotriges.

The warriors from Brittany who ruled them, and the Belgae farther east who finally conquered them, were not the only groups of people to be driven across from Gaul in these times. There were also minor groups, and these included immigrants who had something of their own to contribute to the growth of the old La Tène style into a distinctively British Celtic art.

The scribing of geometrical forms of La Tène design on pottery with compasses, helped out by small circle-stamps, was practised in parts of Brittany before Caesar's conquest, and rather similar designs were now brought over, to the Glastonbury lake-village (Fig. 16) and other places, notably in East Sussex and parts of Kent. Their influence probably helped the development of the curving La Tène scroll-patterns into a purely geometrical style. In this style, on pottery and still more strikingly on fine bronze-work, we find the unfaltering curves and circles of such designs set off by hatching with the look of basketry – though it was more probably inspired by the stitchery of gay textiles, which themselves, of course, have perished. The best-established schools of fine bronze-work in Britain were in the northern and eastern territories, where the La Tène style had been implanted by the Parisi and their like (p. 133), but this geometric tendency was furthered from the south, and the results appear in various regions, especially along the connecting line across the Midlands (p. 145) between south-west and north-east.

They appear on ornamented sword-scabbards, as found at Hunsbury (p. 145) and in Somerset near the Meare lake-village, and on a number of smaller things, but most perfectly on the bronze mirrors which we spoke of in the last chapter. Their engraved backs show a varied range of these ingenious spreading curve-patterns, but the most successful are those from Desborough in the Midlands (Fig. 19) and Birdlip at the Cotswold edge above Gloucester, in which symmetry keeps the design from straggling without spoiling its grace. As time went on, symmetry became more and more sought after, and it is not hard to see in this the first-fruits of a new influence in British art, the classical influence of Rome. For Gaul was now a Roman province, and in the last twenty years before Christ renewed contacts across the Channel began to bring that influence in. One can admire it, rendered in skilfully cast relief, in the taut, springy formality of our great masterpiece, the shield found in the Thames at Battersea (Pl. 13). But in some of the mirrors it is less admirable, and the nature of its effects can be judged particularly well in the school of ornament centred among the Belgae, which specialized not in line-drawing on metal so much as in enamel-work. In earlier times enamel had been an attached embellishment on metal-work, like the coral which it imitated, but the Belgic craftsmen poured it molten into prepared spaces in their designs, at first in roundels of various kinds like those on the Battersea shield, and then in hollowed-out fields in the ornamental surface itself. Their enamel colour was red, which contrasted showily with the yellow of the bronze; but the effect of Roman influence on their designs was to make them more tidy and correct-looking, like that of the harness-mount from Polden Hill on the Somerset

FIG. 19. The Desborough mirror,
showing the engraved ornament of the back.

edge of western Belgic territory (Pl. 11B), and in the end
fussy or merely clever.

But we have not yet reached the last years of British independence to which these pieces belong. For two full genera-

tions from about 20 B.C. the power of the Belgic kingdoms in the south of Britain grew, and rivalry and conflict sharpened, especially between that founded by Commius south of the Thames and that of the successors of Cassivellaunus north of it. Commius had three sons, and their history can be made out in some sort from their coins, which can be arranged in order of age in their various districts, and almost from the outset show the influence of Roman models. The dominion of Cassivellaunus in Hertfordshire descended to a king named Tasciovanus; his coinage, showing the same influence in its own way, was minted mainly at Verulamium, the settlement by St Albans where he had his chief capital. The terms imposed by Caesar were a dead letter now, and he soon resumed aggression against the Trinovantes, which reached its goal when he died about A.D. 10. For his son at once attacked their king (who took refuge with the Roman emperor Augustus) and annexed their capital and lands. The capital was named Camulodunum, where now is Colchester in north-east Essex, and the son, who became the greatest of the British kings, was named Cunobelin – the Cymbeline of Shakespeare's play.

This act of conquest had far-reaching consequences. The Trinovantes had already received Belgic culture and settlers from Kent, and when Cunobelin combined their territory with all his father's dominions he was master of a large and solid kingdom. By about A.D. 25 he had added to it all Kent, and carried his frontier on the north and west to the edge of the Fens and across Northants and Oxfordshire to the Thames, which divided him from the rival kingdom of the house of Commius. At first sight his capital far away in Essex seems an odd choice, but the Colne estuary made Colchester a port, and under him it quickly attracted trade with the Roman Empire across the Narrow Seas. It was now, too, that the first small trading-station was established, probably by Roman merchants, on the site of London. A great military disaster in A.D. 9 had broken the Romans' plan of conquering Germany, and for their merchants the growth of commerce with Cunobelin's Britain could partly offset the loss of German markets. The Britons exported corn and cattle, metals and also slaves – the captives of their wars, whose iron shackles have several times been found – and received as imports luxuries such as glass and fine pottery, which prepared their material culture for its predestined end – absorption in the Roman Empire itself.

These foreign goods – red-glazed pottery from Italy and its imitations from Belgic Gaul, the great jars which held southern wine, and ornaments such as brooches and the like – have been found in plenty in the central area of Cunobelin's capital, which lay just outside modern Colchester looking onto the river; the native products, pottery above all, were profoundly affected by their example, and on this mounting material civilization the British king grew rich. And on the excellent coinage which he minted, in gold, silver, and bronze, the designs show a positive invasion of Britain by Roman art. The full extent of Camulodunum was immense, though its inhabited areas were scattered, and it was defended on the landward side by line upon line of great dykes of earthwork, much of which may still be seen. Near one of these, at Lexden, was a cemetery of many graves, and here stands a huge barrow, which has been excavated and found to contain a mass of furnishings for the splendour of the dead. There seems to have been a great funeral bier of wood and iron, with lavish ornaments of enamel-studded bronze; the many bronze objects include statuettes in almost wholly classical style, and there was actually a silver portrait-medallion of the Roman Emperor Augustus, made from a coin. This may, indeed, well be the sepulchre of Cunobelin himself.

Exactly what religious beliefs were bound up with such funeral rites is difficult to say, but it appears here, as in many Celtic graves, particularly on the Continent, that grave-goods had been damaged so that they too should be accounted dead, and thus be available for their owner's use beyond the grave. As we have seen, the bodies of the dead were now cremated, and it was certainly the disembodied soul of a man which was held immortal: its passage at death into a new and different body was part of the doctrine taught by the powerful Celtic priesthood of both Gaul and Britain, the order of the Druids. Caesar and other writers have left an account of the Druids which has appealed greatly to people's imagination, and at one time almost every prehistoric monument was thought to be 'Druidical'. Actually their human burnt-offerings, their blood-sacrifices, their divination, their philosophy and their power as teachers and judges are difficult to place in a modern account of ancient Britain, mainly because the religious monuments of the Iron Age, when they flourished, are so little known. It seems probable that their lore combined traditions coming from a wide range of origins: the cutting of the mistletoe on the sacred oak, for example, was a German as well as a Celtic ceremony, though the golden sickle they are said to have used was perhaps directly descended from the sickles of the Bronze Age in Britain and Gaul. But their development as an organized priesthood seems confined to these western lands, and probably has at least some of its roots in the religious life of the Bronze Age. We have seen that in that life elements brought in by the Beaker and other invaders blended with the mysterious cults of the megalith-builders (p. 58). Thus, while it is quite wrong to think of Stonehenge as properly a 'Druids' Temple', it appears that the Druids did use Stonehenge, for, as has already been pointed out (p. 80), outside the stone circles there emplacements for two more circles have been found, which seem to be additions made at some time in the Iron Age. And near Frilford in Berkshire remains of a little Iron Age sanctuary have lately been excavated which looks very like a shrunken and distorted version of an Early Bronze Age 'henge'. Druidism, in fact, though its institutions probably differed in different parts of Britain as regards details, was compounded with ancient elements which the whole land, for all its multitude of gods and goblins, held to some extent in common. And thus it must have been something of a unifying force among the Britons, in an age when local tribes and cultures, invading or invaded, were making such a welter of strife with one another.

The strife was not confined to the frontiers between the Belgae and their neighbours. We have already seen how Cunobelin extended his kingdom by war. Later he seems to have sent his sons with expeditions across the Thames, to carve out princedoms from the lands of the house of Commius. Another expedition had started westwards across north Oxfordshire, where Belgic dyke-building is again in evidence in Blenheim Park, to reach the Cotswolds at Bourton-on-the-Water. And the Belgae south of the Thames were also striking west, reaching now beyond Maiden Castle to Hembury Fort in Devon, assailing the Glastonbury lake-village, and probably climbing the Mendips and the hills past Bath and Bristol. The great stone-walled fort of Worlebury at Weston-super-Mare has yielded many skulls and bones from a massacre, and at Bredon Hill fort, on the far edge of the Cotswolds, the main entrance of about this time has been found choked with the grisly remains of another, in which the victims' bodies had been hacked to pieces and their heads lined up on the gate to burn and crash with it to the ground. And the tremendous hill-forts beyond the Severn, through Herefordshire and all up the Marches of Wales, were built and rebuilt, sometimes on a colossal scale, in a way which shows clearly enough that the Iron Age of Britain had become truly an age of iron.

Migrations of peoples in the west went far. Along much of the west of Scotland there are signs that people now were coming up from the south, though indeed beyond a few bone weaving-tools and the like there is little for us now to recognize them by, except the small, strong ring-forts of their chiefs, underground galleries like the Cornish fogou (p. 138), and structures developed from the Cornish courtyard house, which they seemingly brought with them. But these in the far north inspired the growth of veritable castles, the towering stone structures known as brochs (Fig. 20), with stairs and chambers in the thickness of their walls, and an open court within – their whole design proclaiming them the strongholds of a people bred to raiding and fighting by sea and land. Probably more of such migrations affected Ireland too. Though their material remains are as yet lacking, the oldest epic tales of Irish literature reach back to this stage, and tell of a world as full of the noise of battle as it is full of mystery and magic.

Fighting was, indeed, an accepted part of men's lives in the ancient world, in civilized Greece no less than in barbaric Britain. But to both there came a time when war became more than an occasional affair between high-spirited neighbours, and threatened to grow into a perpetual curse. That time came when the pattern of society became too unbalanced for the normal tenor of peace to be maintained, so that war ceased to be a local adjustment of forces, and began to throw the pattern still farther out of balance. New forces were at work, which the old simple forms of society could not control. The Greek city states could never for long unite, and the civilization they had done so much to create came to demand their merging in something bigger. At long last that something turned into the Roman Empire, and now it was

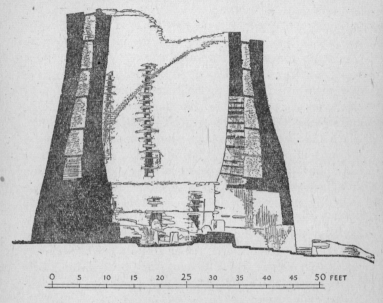

FIG. 20. The Broch of Mousa, Shetland: sectional view showing the stairs and galleries in the walls of the stone tower.

the Roman Empire that came to merge in itself the tribal disunion of Britain.

The Belgic kingdoms had certainly succeeded in merging lesser tribes, and Cunobelin's was something approaching a national state. But it was the creation of one man, and both the force and the wealth which made the Belgic power rested on their culture's borrowings from the higher civilization overseas. It was not long before the higher civilization was ready to call for the payment of its debts. Caesar had underrated his task, and had come and gone too soon; but close on a hundred years later the Roman Empire judged that the time was ripe. Soon after A.D. 40 Cunobelin was dead, and his kingdom in turmoil. From his successors' violence the last of the sons of Commius fled to Rome, and the new emperor Claudius saw that the situation demanded a response. Britain was disunited, and had wealth in plenty for exploiting: he had the legions and the ships, and he wanted the laurels of a conquest.

He got them. In the year A.D. 43 a strong Roman army landed on the coast of Kent, and soon Camulodunum surrendered. After forty years of gradual advance by the Romans, their general Agricola at last reached the gate of the Scottish Highlands, and broke in one battle the gathered clans of the northern Britons. But he got no farther. The effort for the Empire was too great, the Highlands were too unrewarding, and the Roman Government thought it best to call a halt. In another forty years there had been a retreat, and Hadrian was building his famous Wall from Tyneside to the Solway. Basing his frontier on that line, he accepted the impossibility of going permanently beyond it, and so it came about that while all the richer lands to the south remained a Roman province, beyond the Wall Prehistoric Britain lived on. Not three centuries from Agricola's day, the Picts and Scots were carrying their warfare back into the province's heart, joining hands with the Saxon invaders from over the North Sea. Soon after A.D. 400 Roman rule in this island was over. And in the 'Dark Ages' which followed, the England, Wales, and Scotland of familiar history were born, with the legacy of Prehistoric Britain, both in war and peace, as a vital part of their inheritance.

Tailpiece

WE started with ape-men, and have ended with Anglo-Saxons. The human history of the half a million or so intervening years has been told, sketchily and laconically in its early parts, but with increasing detail and accuracy. After the first chapter – that is to say, after Britain assumed its island form – the reader may well have been irked by a certain repetitiveness in the story. Chapter after chapter, almost page after page, has shown a recurring theme: the invasion of that island from the Continent. The impact of these waves of invasion beats monotonously through the narrative From Spain and the Mediterranean, from northern France, the Low Countries and Scandinavia they roll, each, when it arrives, sweeping over a lesser or a greater part of Britain and altering its character. Often before it reaches the highland zone the force of the wave is spent and it breaks up on the mountain scarps to filter more weakly into the regions beyond.

As writers we regret this monotony, but as prehistorians we cannot alter it. Such was the pattern of British prehistory, a pattern made inevitable by Britain's position as a fertile island accessible to a restless Continental population.

To many the number of these prehistoric incursions may be new and surprising. They may feel incredulous and suspect them to be creations of the archaeologist's imagination. But see how uninterruptedly they run on into historic times, when each has a proper name attached and seems not incredible at all, but simple and familiar. We all know 1066, and before that it was the Danes and Norsemen, then the Anglo-Saxons, the rather different invasion of the Romans, and before them the earliest historically recorded incursion, that of the Belgae. There is no break in continuity and no difference of character between these immigrations and the nameless ones that preceded them. Indeed, the archaeological method has, of course, been applied to the historical invasions, and has given substance and precision to scanty and inaccurate written records.

If this account of early Britain has been monotonous, it has also, we are only too well aware, been full of gaps. These will many of them be closed during the next decade, if anything so essentially peaceable as archaeological research is possible in those years. In the present century knowledge has accumulated at an astonishing speed. It was not at first merely a question of closing gaps, but of setting up the bare framework; incomplete though our information remains, it is immense when compared with the blank which confronted our immediate ancestors when they tried to look back beyond the Roman conquest. A century ago the whole of the time covered by this book was a void vaguely peopled with 'ancient Britons', while the idea that any of these shadowy characters should have been about before 4004 would have seemed dubious to all and blasphemous to many. How and by what manner of men has this information been won? An interest in his own past is perhaps not unexpected in man; it is an obvious field for the exercise of his eternal curiosity, his desire to know. But intellectual inquisitiveness is not the only incentive. There are also the childish pleasures of treasure-seeking which can be given a grown-up form by the cloak of archaeology, and the passion of many individuals for amassing a collection of objects. We have even been told by psychologists that the pursuit of prehistory really represents a striving to return to the womb. These various urges, then, have prompted a number of men and women to devote much time and toil to searching out the remains of the past that survive on and under the surface of their country.

The pioneers were men who travelled the countryside to further the topographical studies which were among the enthusiasms of the English Renaissance. Conspicuous among them was Leland, who in the time of Henry VIII toured England and recorded what he saw of her antiquities, generally medieval castles, abbeys and the like, but including among them such conspicuous prehistoric monuments as caught his eye and his interest. The Elizabethan age produced Camden, who in 1586 published his bulky volume, *Britannia*, in which was collected a mass of material from medieval writings, but also facts and speculations concerning prehistory. The outstanding figure of the seventeenth century was John Aubrey, an itinerant after the manner of Leland, whose careful field notes are still of the greatest value to present-day students. Even Defoe, preoccupied though he was with commerce, paused to comment on such famous sites as Stonehenge, and incidentally to rebuke the antiquaries of his day for their habit of idle speculation.

All these earlier workers can be seen as the harbingers of the outburst of antiquarian fervour which was one of the results of that great revolution in taste and cultural values, the Romantic Movement. Many of us must have stumbled upon one of those gloomy, dripping and uncomfortable grottoes dear to the eighteenth- and early nineteenth-century landscape gardener, and read the verses in praise of caves and hermits and ivy inscribed on their walls. To the macabre and morbid side of the Movement prehistoric antiquity was bound to appeal; it could contribute the 'sightless skulls and crumbling bones', the altar stones on which blood might have flowed and victims writhed in 'horrid', fascinating anguish. Above all, it offered a setting for the 'white-haired

Druid bard sublime'. The great champion and popularizer of the Druids was William Stukeley, a leader during the earlier phase of the Romantic Movement. In the first decade of the eighteenth century, when he was studying medicine and developing his strong scientific bent, one would have thought him a legitimate child of the Age of Reason, yet he was to end his days as one of the most fantastical of Romantics. Archaeology was at first but one of the many scientific interests which prompted him to keep smelly anatomical specimens in his room at Cambridge and alarm the college with sudden explosions. After 1718, however, when he became first secretary of the newly-formed Society of Antiquaries, it preoccupied him more and more exclusively. At first he used his scientific training to carry out accurate field work, and in particular to survey and plan all the complexities of Avebury and Stonehenge. But gradually another side of his nature better suited to the Romantic taste asserted itself; he grew increasingly fascinated by the Druids, and conceived that he had a mission to reconcile and relate their supposed doctrines with Christianity, and above all with the conception of the Trinity. This change of heart it was which led him to build extravagant theories on the sober and sound foundations of his earlier work at Avebury and Stonehenge, to see in their stone rings and avenues 'a snake proceeding from a circle . . . the eternal procession of the Son from the First Cause'.

Antiquarianism was now the fashion; young gentlemen rode about the country in search of the Gothick and any remains of the more remote past that might present themselves. Landowners began to concern themselves with the monuments they found on their estates. The results of the fashion ranged in value from the accurate and exhaustive account of Wiltshire antiquities left by Sir Richard Colt Hoare to the mischievous pillaging of barrows undertaken by a number of gentlemen whose names it is kinder to forget. One among them, rather later, whose ravages can be forgiven him because they were both trivial and picturesque, deserves special place. When this antiquary wished to secure for his collection the contents of a barrow that stood on the property of another, he appeared on the site in an ample cloak and settled down as though to rest or contemplate the beauties of rugged nature. In reality, however, his hands were feverishly busy under the folds of his cloak, excavating the grave and assembling the booty.

As the nineteenth century advanced the social status of archaeology gradually changed in accordance with the changing structure of English society. The power of the upper classes to act as sole arbiters of taste and fashion was slipping from them as the rising middle class assumed control. We find archaeological research passing into the hands of professional or retired business men, and in those hands it was inevitable and right, if a little sad, that the subject should grow more sober and scientific, more in harmony with the gospel of the Prince Consort than it had been in its extravagant youth as a standard-bearer of the Romantic Movement.

In a purely practical way, too, the Industrial Revolution affected archaeology. Never before had the soil of England been so perpetually disturbed, so deeply cut about by the hand of man. Every time that a bank or a factory went up, a canal or railway line was driven, or a quarry sunk, there was good chance that some long-hidden antiquity might be uncovered. To house all these finds, and others the fruits of deliberate archaeological excavation, the middle class subscribed its money to build museums in provincial towns, for it usually lacked both the arrogance and the means which had enabled the eighteenth-century antiquaries to install their collections in their own mansions.

As well as museums, local antiquarian societies were founded. All over the countryside they sprang up, with an enthusiastic membership of squires and doctors and parsons, interested ladies and a few noblemen, all eager to attend and give lectures and to make delightful excursions into the country, armed with notebooks and picnic hampers. It is easy to laugh at them, but these societies have given and continue to give invaluable service to learning. Let anyone who encounters one of their excursions and watches the party, as it turns out of its buses to stream across fields, crowd over stiles, surge into country houses and toil with limbs often no longer young to the tops of hills, pause and think with some pride of the English tradition which, with all its absurdity, it worthily represents.

Soon after the middle of the nineteenth century archæology was to be profoundly affected by that happening which did more to liberate the human mind than anything since the day when Galileo realized that the earth went round the sun: the formulation by Darwin of the principles of evolution. Less than a century after the publication of the *Origin of Species* in 1859 it is still hard to appreciate what a tremendous striking off of chains that was. While thinking people had not, of course, always shared the general public's complete acceptance of the 'received' story of the creation and Archbishop Ussher's date for it, nevertheless it narrowly circumscribed their thought.

Into the wide vista of speculation and study finally laid open by Darwin and Huxley, no one was more bound to advance than the archaeologist. Man could now be fitted into geological time, and this aspect of archaeological research developed most rapidly. Immediately the Frenchman Boucher de Perthes' claim to have found humanly shaped implements in early gravels became acceptable, and the Neanderthal skull from Gibraltar, which had lain incognito since its discovery in 1848, was hailed as one of the precursors of Adam, a being who could now be recognized by respectable people.

The half-century after the appearance of the *Origin of Species* was a time of steady progress in archaeological studies. Field workers such as Greenwell and Mortimer in Yorkshire and Cunnington in Wiltshire laboured to produce a mass of factual material on which classifications and generalizations could gradually be built. The great Manchester professor Boyd Dawkins did much to reconcile the geological approaches to archaeology with the humanistic.

Overtopping them all was an unusual and latterly eccentric figure, a figure great enough to be an exception to the main trend of his times. General Lane Fox Pitt-Rivers was a man who would seem more in place among eighteenth-century antiquaries. After a career as a Guards officer he inherited vast estates round Cranborne Chase; he could ride, it was said, from Rushmore to the sea without leaving his own land. Cranborne Chase is scattered with antiquities of many kinds, and the General was now able to satisfy the interest in primitive material culture and excavation which had hitherto been only an immense spare-time hobby. He had many greater eccentricities. He planted his grounds with exotic trees and shrubs and filled them with alarmingly exotic animals, and on Sundays obliged his tenants to come to listen to the brass band which played in his 'Larmer Tree Grounds'. When excavating he would drive off to the site in a high dogcart, accompanied by his carefully trained assistants, perched on penny-farthing bicycles, and displaying the General's colours round the brims of their boater hats. This man, who is personally so reminiscent of the eighteenth century, was, in fact, the immediate inspiration of the scientific archaeology of the twentieth. In the objectivity and detail of his excavation and the exhaustiveness of his publication he has never been outdone. His vast *Excavations on Cranborne Chase*, which appeared between 1887 and 1898, is in most respects a model of what such a publication should be when money is unlimited. In the private museum on his estate models were not only carved from solid mahogany, but were of meticulous accuracy. As a reward, his work can still be used to-day, often to support ideas of which he could have no conception.

The present century has seen another great change in prehistoric studies. Hitherto, as we have shown, it had not been the academic scholars who were interested in prehistory, nor yet the scientists, apart from its purely geological aspects, but the gentry, and then also the professional men, the parsons, lawyers and doctors, whose affairs took them out of doors. But now more and more scholars, led by the Hellenists, began to concern themselves with barbarian archaeology, while, on the other hand, laboratory methods were utilized to make it more scientific. As the subject in this way grew increasingly wide and complex, it demanded to become a full-time study. While amateurs still make invaluable contributions to archaeology, its leaders are now professionals working at universities and museums. Probably past Fellows of the Society of Antiquaries would be shocked at the young men and women who sit on their red-leather benches to-day, people who use the study of antiquity as a means of earning their bread, and not as a cultivated pastime and opportunity for unrestrained speculation. But they would have to recognize that their achievements in recent years have been very great. Co-operation with classical scholarship is at last bridging the senseless gap which long divided Greek and Roman from prehistoric studies, so that we begin to get a unified picture of the classical and barbarian peoples who shared Europe and who impinged upon one

another so often. Simultaneously the introduction of ingenious analytical techniques of the laboratory makes it
reasonable for archaeology to claim to be in many respects
an exact science.

Happily the result of all this has not been to make the
subject increasingly academic and difficult. On the contrary,
it has made it possible to get much nearer to early man, to
see him as an individual, as a member of society, to divine
something of his ways of thought and his emotions. It has
been the main object of this small book to give some hints
of this achievement to a wider public.

Bibliography

The list is for the most part limited to books published in the last twenty years. Simpler and more inexpensive books are marked*.

GENERAL

Prehistory and Civilization:

*V. GORDON CHILDE, *Man Makes Himself.* London: Watts, 1936. (Thinker's Library), 1939.

*V. GORDON CHILDE, *What Happened in History.* (Pelican Books, A 108.) Harmondsworth: Penguin Books, 1942.

*GRAHAME CLARK (J. G. D.), *Archæology and Society*, 2nd edition, London: Methuen, 1946.

EUROPE

C. S. COON, *The Races of Europe.* New York: Macmillan, 1939.

C. F. C. HAWKES, *The Prehistoric Foundations of Europe: to the Mycenean Age.* London: Methuen, 1940.

*EDITH PLANT, *Man's Unwritten Past.* (Realms of Natural Science Series.) Oxford University Press (London: Milford), 1942.

Palaeolithic:

*M. C. BURKITT, *The Old Stone Age.* Cambridge University Press, 1933.

*W. B. WRIGHT, *Tools and the Man.* London: Bell, 1939.

*DOROTHY DAVISON, *Men of the Dawn.* London: Watts (Thinker's Library), 1934.

Mesolithic:

J. G. D. CLARK, *The Mesolithic Settlement of Northern Europe.* Cambridge University Press, 1936.

Mesolithic to Bronze Age:

V. GORDON CHILDE, *The Dawn of European Civilization* (2nd edn.). London: Kegan Paul, 1939.

BIBLIOGRAPHY

BRITAIN
(mainly Mesolithic onwards)

*V. GORDON CHILDE, *Prehistoric Communities of the British Isles.* London and Edinburgh: Chambers, 1940.
At present the standard work: contains full earlier bibliography.

*SIR CYRIL FOX, *The Personality of Britain: its Influence on Inhabitant and Invader in Prehistoric and Early Historic Times* (4th edn., 1943).

*JACQUETTA AND CHRISTOPHER HAWKES, *Prehistoric Britain* (an extended version of the present work). London: Chatto and Windus, 1947.

*JACQUETTA HAWKES, *A Guide to the Prehistoric and Roman Monuments of England and Wales.* London: Chatto & Windus, 1951.

*JACQUETTA HAWKES, *Early Britain.* Collins, 1944.

*STUART PIGGOTT, *British Prehistory.* Oxford University Press, 1949.

England:

*GRAHAME CLARK (J. G. D.) *Prehistoric England.* London: Batsford, 1940.

Wales:

*W. F. GRIMES, *A Guide to the Collection Illustrating the Prehistory of Wales.* Cardiff: National Museum of Wales, 1939.

Scotland:

V. GORDON CHILDE, *The Prehistory of Scotland.* London: Kegan Paul, 1935.

*V. GORDON CHILDE, *Prehistoric Scotland.* (Historical Association Pamphlets, no. 115). London: Bell, 1940.

*V. GORDON CHILDE, *Scotland before the Scots.* London: Methuen, 1945.

176

BIBLIOGRAPHY

Special Counties:

*W. J. VARLEY AND J. WILFRID JACKSON, *Prehistoric Cheshire*.
(Handbook to the History of Cheshire, no. 1.) Chester: Cheshire
Rural Community Council, 1940.

*M. E. CUNNINGTON, *An Introduction to the Archæology of Wilt-shire* (3rd edn.). Devizes: Woodward, 1934.

*E. CECIL CURWEN, *The Archæology of Sussex*. (County Archæologies Series.) London: Methuen, 1937.

*Other volumes in the County Archæologies Series (London:
Methuen) are:

H. J. E. PEAKE, *The Archæology of Berkshire*, 1930.

H. O'NEILL HENCKEN, *The Archæology of Cornwall and Scilly*,
1932.

R. F. JESSUP, *The Archæology of Kent*, 1930.

C. E. VULLIAMY, *The Archæology of Middlesex and London*, 1930.

DINA P. DOBSON, *The Archæology of Somerset*, 1931.

F. AND H. W. ELGEE, *The Archæology of Yorkshire*, 1932.

Special Sites (including some books earlier than 1933):

*FRANK STEVENS, *Stonehenge: To-day and Yesterday*. (The Official
Guide to Stonehenge.) London: H.M. Stationery Office (latest
edn.), 1938.

*A. BULLEID, *The Lake-Villages of Somerset*. (Somerset Folk Series,
no. 16.) London: Folk Press (2nd edition), 1948.

A. BULLEID AND H. ST GEORGE GRAY, *The Glastonbury Lake-Village*. Glastonbury Antiquarian Society (Barnicott and Pearce
printers, Taunton), 2 vols., 1911–17.

Reports of the Research Committee of the Society of Antiquaries:

R. E. M. AND T. V. WHEELER, *Verulamium: a Belgic and two
Roman Cities*. Oxford University Press (London: Milford), 1936.

R. E. M. WHEELER, *Maiden Castle*. Oxford University Press
(London: Cumberlege), 1943.

C. F. C. HAWKES AND M. R. HULL, *Camulodunum*. Oxford
University Press (London: Cumberlege), 1947.

BIBLIOGRAPHY

Later Iron Age: Roman Britain:

Art:

E. THURLOW LEEDS, *Celtic Ornament (to* A.D. 700). Oxford: Clarendon Press, 1933.

General:

*R. G. COLLINGWOOD, *Roman Britain* (latest edn.). Oxford: Clarendon Press, 1934.

R. G. COLLINGWOOD AND J. N. L. MYRES, *Roman Britain and the English Settlements.* (The Oxford History of England, Vol. 1: 2nd edn.) Oxford: Clarendon Press, 1936.

*IAN RICHMOND, *Roman Britain* (Britain in Pictures Series). London: Collins, 1947.

Illustrated Regional Guides to Ancient Monuments, H.M. Office of Works:

*Vol. I, *Northern England*
*Vol. II, *Southern England*
*Vol. III, *E. Anglia and Midlands*
*Vol. IV, *South Wales.*
    London: H.M. Stationery Office, 1935–9.

Field Archaeology, Maps, and Air-Photography (including some publications earlier than 1933):

R. J. C. ATKINSON, *Field Archæology*, London: Methuen, 1946.

Ordnance Survey publications: London, H.M. Stationery Office:
Field Archæology (notes for beginners). 2nd edn., 1936.

Maps:

General Map of the major visible antiquities of Great Britain older than A.D. 1066:

Ancient Britain: (1) *North Sheet*, (2) *South Sheet*. Scale, 10 miles to inch. 1st edn., 1951.

Megalithic Survey (maps, ¼ mile to inch, showing distribution of long barrows, megaliths, dwelling-sites, flint-mines, with lists and explanatory text), comprising:

Map of Neolithic Wessex.

Map of the Trent Basin.

Map of South Wales.

BIBLIOGRAPHY

Celtic Earthworks of Salisbury Plain (maps, 1: 25,000, showing Celtic fields, earthworks, and barrows: one so far published):

Old Sarum (map covering the district around). Revised edn., 1937.

Period Map (with explanatory letterpress):

Roman Britain. 2nd edn., 1931.

Air-Photography (author, O. G. S. Crawford):

Air-Photography and Archæology. (Wessex district: illustrated with air-photographs and maps), 2nd edn., 1928.

Air-Photography for Archæologists (the subject illustrated by typical examples). 1929.

O. G. S. CRAWFORD AND A. KEILLER, *Wessex from the Air*. Oxford: Clarendon Press, 1928.

PERIODICALS

General quarterly review of archaeology, equally for the specialist and the ordinary reader:

Antiquity, edited by O. G. S. Crawford and published by H. W. Edwards, The Wharf, Newbury, Berks; appears regularly in March, June, September and December.

General monthly:

The Archaeological News Letter. London, 273 Grays Inn Road. Has appeared each month since April, 1948.

Journals published by Societies:

The Prehistoric Society:

Proceedings of the Prehistoric Society, edited by J. G. D. Clark (University Museum of Archaeology and Ethnology, Downing Street, Cambridge). Contains, in addition to articles, a full summary account of each year's excavations; appears normally half-yearly.

Society for the Promotion of Roman Studies (50 Bedford Square, London, WC1):

The Journal of Roman Studies. Contains, in addition to articles, a full summary account of each year's excavations: may include prehistoric (usually Iron Age) as well as Roman material; appears normally half-yearly.

179

BIBLIOGRAPHY

The following are concerned with archaeology of both prehistoric and later periods:

Society of Antiquaries (Burlington House, London, W1):

The Antiquaries Journal (normally quarterly).

Archaeologia (normally a large annual volume).

Royal Archaeological Institute (Lancaster House, London, SW1):

The Archaeological Journal (normally half-yearly).

Wales: Cambrian Archaeological Association (Whitford, Holywell, Flints.):

Archæologia Cambrensis (normally half-yearly).

Scotland: Society of Antiquaries of Scotland (Edinburgh):
Proceedings of the Society (an annual volume).

Most English counties have an archaeological society normally publishing a journal annually (a few more often).

The Congress of Archaeological Societies (in union with the Society of Antiquaries: Burlington House, London, W1) published a small annual *Report of the Research Committee* of the Congress, which gave a summary account of all discoveries made during the year, and a bibliography of all articles in periodicals, and principal books, published relating to Prehistoric, Roman, post-Roman, and Medieval archaeology, for the whole of the British Isles. This appeared to 1939 inclusive.

A similar publication, the *Archaeological Bulletin for the British Isles*, has now been undertaken by the Congress's successor, the Council for British Archaeology (c/o London University Institute of Archaeology, Inner Circle, Regent's Park, London, N.W.1): the first issue, covering 1940–46, appeared in 1949, and is being followed by annual issues for 1947 and each following year.

The Council has also published, in 1948, a handbook entitled *Archæology in Great Britain: Survey and Policy of Field Research* (*Part I, to the Seventh Century A.D.*).

Index

INDEX

THE ARCHAEOLOGY OF PALESTINE

W. F. Albright

A 199

This book and *Prehistoric India* by Professor Stuart Piggott (which will be reprinted shortly) are the first two volumes in a new series, The Pelican Archaeologies, under the general editorship of M. E. L. Mallowan, Professor of Western Asiatic Archaeology in the University of London.

The tiny country on the Eastern Mediterranean coast which has played so outstanding a part in human history has yielded up in recent years so many of the secrets of its past that a popular summary of the results has long been overdue. Professor Albright, who has himself done so much to bring the treasures of its past to light, here tells the story of their gradual unearthing, of the building up of a connected picture of Palestine's history, and of the light thus thrown on human history in general and on the Old Testament story.

Archaeological Books by
Sir Leonard Woolley

*

UR OF THE CHALDEES
A27

An account of the excavations that have taken place in Ur over a number of years, and particularly the recent expeditions sponsored by the University Museum of Pennsylvannia and the British Museum under the directorship of the author of this book.

Time and Tide said: 'Reading *Ur of the Chaldees* one is filled with awe at the richness and perfection of man's workmanship 5,000 years ago; at the immensity of man's knowledge to-day in piecing together the scattered remains of the past.' (1s 6d)

DIGGING UP THE PAST
A4

In this Pelican Sir Leonard Woolley explains in detail what archaeology is all about, describing the preliminary organization of a 'dig', the delicate processes of getting inside a site, and the subsequent analysis of the evidence which has been brought to light. The text is illustrated by a fine series of plates covering many of the processes and the discoveries of archaeology in Ur, Italy, Palestine, Knossos, Egypt and Scandinavia. (1s 6d)

*

Peoples of Britain

The following have been published in the Pelican series: *The Scots* by Moray McLaren (A 256), *The Irish* by Sean O'Faolain (A184), and *The Welsh* by Wyn Griffiths (A 215). They give concise accounts of the history, culture and character of these peoples.

Other Pelicans

*

WHAT HAPPENED IN HISTORY

V. Gordon Childe

A 108

Professor Gordon Childe discusses the changes in material well-being and mental outlook which took place throughout the pre-historic and early historic ages up to the break-up of the Roman Empire. (2s 6d)

BEFORE PHILOSOPHY

H. and H. A. Frankfort, J. Wilson and T. Jacobsen

A 198

An analysis of the myths which for Ancient Man represented his peculiar form of concrete thought concerning the problems of self and the universe, his moral and religious preoccupations.

PRIMITIVE ART

Leonhard Adam

A 67

This is a revised and enlarged edition of a work specially written for Pelican Books, which describes the various forms which the artistic impulse has taken among primitive peoples – from the Stone Age men who roamed the plains of Europe twenty thousand years ago to the modern Negro inventing new ways of carving the human figure among the forests of the Ivory Coast. (2s 6d)

The Pelican History of England

*

While each volume is complete in itself, this whole series has been planned to provide an intelligent and consecutive guide to the development of English society in all its aspects. Of the eight volumes, five are already available:

TUDOR ENGLAND – *S. T. Bindoff, Professor of History at Queen Mary College, London*

ENGLAND IN THE EIGHTEENTH CENTURY – *J. H. Plumb, Fellow of Christ's College, Cambridge*

ENGLAND IN THE NINETEENTH CENTURY (1815–1914) – *David Thomson, Fellow of Sidney Sussex College, Cambridge*

THE BEGINNINGS OF ENGLISH SOCIETY (from the Anglo-Saxon Invasion) – *Dorothy Whitelock, Fellow of St Hilda's College, Oxford*

ENGLISH SOCIETY IN THE EARLY MIDDLE AGES, 1066–1307 – *Doris Mary Stenton, Lecturer at Reading University*

The others, which will follow as soon as possible, are:

ROMAN BRITAIN – *Professor Ian Richmond, King's College, Newcastle-on-Tyne*

ENGLAND IN THE LATE MIDDLE AGES – *A. R. Myers, Lecturer at Liverpool University*

ENGLAND IN THE SEVENTEENTH CENTURY – *Maurice Ashley, M.A.*

The Pelican Philosophies

*

A new series of Pelicans on Philosophy has been planned under
the General Editorship of A. J. Ayer, Grote Professor of the
Philosophy of Mind and Logic at University College, London. It
will comprise books on the individual philosophers, ancient,
medieval and modern as well as Introductions to Philosophy,
Logic, Ethics, Political Philosophy and the Philosophy of Science.
The first two volumes, which have been published recently, are:

PEIRCE AND PRAGMATISM – *Professor W. B. Gallie, of University College, North Staffordshire*

SPINOZA – *Stuart Hampshire, Fellow of New College, Oxford*

Among other volumes in active preparation are:

BUTLER'S MORAL PHILOSOPHY – *Austin Duncan-Jones, of
Birmingham University*

J. S. MILL – *Karl Britton, of University College, Swansea*

LOCKE – *Professor J. J. O'Connor of the University of Natal,
Pietermaritzburg, South Africa*

*

A companion series of Pelicans on Psychology has recently been
inaugurated under the General Editorship of Professor C. A.
Mace, of Birkbeck College, London. The first two volumes are
William James by Margaret Knight and *The Psychology of the
British Working Man* by Ferdynand Zweig; others are in
preparation.

Ancient Peoples

*

THE AZTECS OF MEXICO
George C. Vaillant
A200

The first British publication of what is still the most important account of the birth and death of one of the world's great civilizations. It contains over 170 half-tone illustrations. *The Scotsman* said – 'Dr Vaillant has re-created vividly the way of life of the Aztecs, their great cities, and their customs and religions. His book is at once a work of deep scholarship and a fascinating story that all can appreciate.'

THE GREEKS
H. D. F. Kitto
A220

A biography and a character-sketch of the Greek people. The author's theme is not what they did, but what they were; in particular, what were the habits of mind and way of life that made their civilization and culture what it was. Raymond Mortimer, reviewing it in the *Sunday Times*, described it as 'the best introduction that I have ever read to Ancient Greece. The author's liveliness of mind and style has enabled him to make a mass of information appetizing and digestible.'

THE ROMANS
R. H. Barrow
A196

'Here is a book which can be thoroughly recommended to teachers who may be looking for a short introduction to the part played by the Romans in the founding of western civilization. He has succeeded in conveying to the modern reader what is best worth remembering about the qualities which make up the genius of the Roman people.' – *The Times Educational Supplement*